POETRY FOR THE ROAD

Published by
George J. Kimble
4941 Hickory Woods East
Antioch TN 37013
www.theroadpoet.com

This book is a work of fiction. Any reference to historical events; to real people, living or dead; or to real locales are intended only to give the fiction a setting in historical reality. Other names, characters, places, and incidents are the product of the author's imagination or are used fictitiously, and any resemblance to real-life people is entirely coincidental.

Kimble, George J.
Poetry For The Road
Copyright 2005
All rights Reserved
Printed in the United States of America

First Edition

ISBN 0-9767024-0-1

POETRY FOR THE ROAD

George J. Kimble

Acknowledgements:

To Dianne Turner for all the encouragement and original artwork. Not to mention her proof reading for hours.
To Al Turner for allowing us to usurp his domicile and still engage us in light conversations.
To Vicki Qualls for contributing her original artwork.
To Mark Qualls for encouraging the first endeavors.
To the Honk Rattle and Roll AACA Touring Club for the inspirations.
To the Nashville Corvette Club for the fellowship and ideas.
To all of those that were friends while I worked on this.
To my wife, Carol, for putting up with The Road Poet all these years.

Dedication

**This book is dedicated to the car enthusiast.
You are the automotive hobby.**

Index of Poetry

Chapter I	Ownership	
Middle Aged And Crazy	(Good Reason for A Corvette)	- 10 -
Negotiating a Dream	(Buying A Car Experience)	- 11 -
Love Your Car	(Friends on New cars)	- 13 -
Black She Devil	(Love Affair with My Corvette)	- 15 -
We Aim To Please	(Dealership Repair Experience)	- 17 -
Shade Tree	(Computerization Of Vehicles)	- 20 -

Chapter II	History of Corvettes	
Classic Glass	(Corvette History)	- 23 -
Instincts Of The Breed	(First NCM Caravan Experience)	- 25 -
Number Five Alive	(C-5 Is Produced)	- 27 -
Beyond Time	(Fifth Anniversary Caravan)	- 30 -
Who Was That Dreamer?	(Salute To The Corvette Father)	- 32 -

Chapter III	A Saga	
Spirit of a Glass Horse	(Willie's Story)	- 35 -
Closing Time	(Angelina's Dream of Willie)	- 38 -
Unlikely Duet	(Roadhouse Encounter)	- 40 -
White Knuckled	(Willie and Angelina Chase)	- 43 -
Bad Mood Rising	(Playboy Attacks)	- 46 -
How Long Is Forever?	(Willie and Angelina Decision)	- 48 -

Chapter IV	Stranger Than Fiction	
Ah!	(Corvette Experienced)	- 52 -
Another Dimension	(Corvette Acts as Time Machine)	- 53 -
Destiny	(Strange End in a Corvette)	- 54 -
Speed Demons	(A Really Bad Dream)	- 56 -
Jagged Edge	(Wrong Exit)	- 58 -

Chapter V	Fantasies	
Hound And The Hare	(Night In The Desert)	- 61 -
110 In The Shade	(Penalty in Louisiana)	- 63 -
Heat Stroke	(Everything Changes)	- 66 -
Plan Brown Rapper	Corvette Street Racer)	- 69 -
Primer Gray After Dark	(Viper Vs. Vette Drag)	- 71 -
Pumping Iron	(Found a Big Block)	- 73 -
Switcharoo	(Making A Ford Go Fast)	- 75 -
Reality Check	(The Perfect Road)	- 77 -
Vette Dreams	(Corvette Sensuality)	- 79 -

Chapter VI	Life Experienced	
What Happened?	(Getting a Kid's First Project)	- 82 -
Quest For The Bubble	(Finding a Special Part)	- 85 -
A Feeling Like This	(Broke Down On The Road)	- 88 -
Poof	(Thieves)	- 90 -
Lifted	(Saved By Angels)	- 93 -
To The Bone	(Snow Driving Experience)	- 96 -

Chapter VII	Shows	
Picture This	(Winter and Restoring)	- 101 -
Udn Udn Inc.	(Restoring Corvette)	- 102 -
Regina	(Trailer Queen Syndrome)	- 104 -
A Glimmer	(Car Show Experience)	- 106 –

Chapter VIII	Road Calls	
Spring Ride	(A Corvette Club Tour)	- 109 -
Clueless	(Lost in the Mountains)	- 111 -
The Sky Is No Limit	(Corvettes Meet Airplanes)	- 114 -
Smokey Mountain Breakdown	(Car Folks Help)	- 117 -
Opportunity	(Bristol Experience)	- 119 -

Chapter IX	Doing It	
Homily of The Rally Master	(Rally Start Instructions)	- 122 -
Some Like It Hot	(Autocross)	- 124 -
Rice Anyone	(A Busting One)	- 125 -
Muscle Vs. Hustle	(Mopar Beats Corvette)	- 128 -

Chapter X	Zoom Zoom Zoom	
Heroes of The Mud	(Dirt Track Memories)	- 132 -
The Test	(Racing Grand Sport)	- 134 -
A Different Battle Scene	(Mosport Race)	- 135 -
Expedition	(Le Mans Race)	- 137 -
The Winner That Lost	(Racer Killed)	- 139 -
Circuit Rap	(The lady's Pit Crew)	- 141 -
Super Stock Racer	(Aged Race Drivers)	- 142 -

Chapter XI	Life, Liberty and Pursuit	
Spinning Out Of Control	(Need a Fast Car)	- 145 -
Defeat The Sinister Ones	(C-5R Is To Win)	- 147 -
Last Chance For Sunoco	(It Was Done)	- 149 -
Specter	(Devil Racing)	- 151 -
Ain't It A Shame	(Bad Wreck Kids)	- 152 -
Walking	(Corvette Brag)	- 154 -

CHAPTER ONE – Ownership

Middle Aged And Crazy	(Good Reason for A Corvette)	- 10 -
Negotiating a Dream	(Buying A Car Experience)	- 11 -
Love Your Car	(Friends on New cars)	- 13-
Black She Devil	(Love Affair with My Corvette)	- 15 -
We Aim To Please	(Dealership Repair Experience)	- 17 -
Shade Tree	(Computerization Of Vehicles)	- 20 -

Middle Aged and Crazy
By George J. Kimble

At middle age I must admit
Life is filled with its struggles
Often times I thought I'd quit
But some things in life are worth the trouble

Went down town and bought a Vette
I don't know if that is good
I didn't do it to win a bet
I just did it, 'cause I could

I drove it fast all day long
It kindled a spark in my spirit
I don't care if that is wrong
Around tight curves I love to steer it

My dear wife opines I'm out of control
I tell her, "It's her big boy's toy"
"To me the Vette's V-8 is visceral"
My family is grown, what is left to enjoy?

Each night when I go to bed
I dream of tomorrow's thrills
My Doctor just shakes with dread
I told him I don't need his pills

Now tonight I may be dead
They won't call me lazy
But on the stone over my head
They'll inscribe Middle Aged and Crazy

Negotiating a Dream
By George J. Kimble

You've done your homework
You're not going to be someone's jerk
You know it's all very important
Now you have to face the Dream Warden

You have counted all your blessings
The dollars and cents you've been checking
You arrive at the shop and everything glistens
You breathe, and notice the Dream Guards listen

Then a charge from a blue suited bull
Asking, "Do you think that model is cool?"
He looks at you as if you are dumb
He points to the row of econo-plums

"Not what you really had in mind"
You are being careful, trying to be kind
You want a roadster, the Corvette car
That's your dream, your shinning star

The dream police are not very nice
Especially when they start talking price
He says," The window sticker is five digits"
He mentions your credit as if you are a midget

You tell him you know, that is only the maker's suggestion
He cringes and coughs like he has congestion
So you give him a bid very plain
And mention the dealership just down the four-lane

"Will you commit to buy today?"
"What did you bring in for a trade?"
Words roll off his tongue like butter off a blade
He is the master of gesture and charade

You catch your reflection in the showroom glass
You ask yourself, "Why am I pleading with this ass?"
Wondering, Is it possible in the grand scheme
To unshackle the Corvette of your dreams

He banters a lot, you shuck and jive
A mutual price has arrived
He swears the Dream Warden won't be pleased
He shakes your hand and gives you the keys

You fill out papers one after another
Crap! They even want the name of your mother!
You feel like he has you in some kind of trance
Back out now, not a chance!

You feel like you've just made your biggest boner
But, at this moment you are the proud owner
Your life savings you have bet
On your dream convertible Corvette

Now the Corvette has been through dealer prep
To its side you float, not step
Oh, the thrill of that first ride
You've gone to heaven, you must have died

Was this all a mistake?
You pinch yourself, you are awake!
Your new Vette is not pretend
Your new Corvette is the living end!

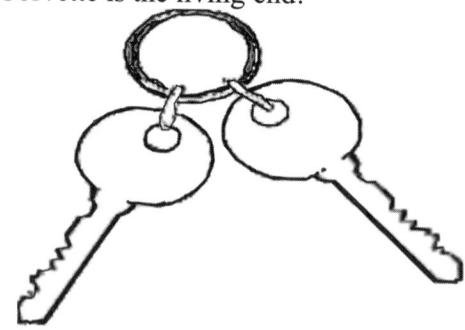

Love Your New Car
By George J. Kimble

A strange encounter in the street
Two ol' buddies happen to meet
Best of friends in times long past
Conversations like these made their friendship last

Hey, my friend, I see you have a new set of wheels
Did you get a really good deal?
You must be really proud of it!
Man, I really love it!

So your car is brand new
Let me suggest some things for you to do
Wouldn't you like to personalize?
Your personality, your machine, should epitomize!

Adding some gusto should be your first inclination
How about a high flow air filter for better acceleration?
Then get the Chip reprogrammed
Get the windows tinted and monogrammed

Install a high power ignition box
Buy a sound system that really rocks
Those factory wheels have gotta go
Put on some chrome five spokes that actually glow

Walk around back and look at this thing
I think you need a giant wing
Put some ground effects on those sides
Pop on some low profile tires, extra wides

For a better exhaust note, get some Corsa tubes
Get a bra, even if there ain't no boobs
Upsize the shocks to reduce body roll
Change the gear set, for coming out of the hole

Now let's see under the hood
Everything there, has to look good
How about bright yellow plug wires
And vacuum hoses too, if you desire?

A lot of those parts you should chrome plate
And powder coated valve covers always look great
Get stainless steel brackets and radiator hose sheaves,
And don't forget, a talking burglar alarm to deter the thieves

Better get a hood with an intake bubble
You can install it, without any trouble
You are gonna need it, when you install that blower
I think your car would look better if it were lowered

Every car needs halogen fog lights
And neon underneath for Cruise-In nights
Racing stripes and a few well placed stickers
Will make your car appear a whole lot quicker

Inside trimmed with yellow and day glow green
Will compliment your new Chameleon paint scheme
When you roll up, it will scream your name!
It will be your claim to fame

Man you are gonna have a blast
Just dig deep and pony up some cash
You will be the high way star
Whenever you have finished your car

Good to see you my friend
Your new car is the living end
I love it
And you should be proud of it

Black She Devil
By George J. Kimble

As I walked from the café
I couldn't take my eyes away
There she sat Black as the Night
The curves of her body meant for delight

That Black She Devil possessed my mind
She shook my soul with a spell of some kind
In my heart I knew it was wrong
I had a dream that lasted all night long

I related this mystical to my brother
I told him , "In my heart there could be no other"
He said, "Now little brother this ain't funny"
"That She Devil will take all your money"

The very next night I had to return
Like a moth to the light I yearned
As I neared from across the street
God, I thought I could feel her heat!

My body with surreal passion shook
As I gave her that fleeting look
I must have been suspended in time
When a man approached her from behind

Like a caress he gently touched her
From that altered state I heard her murmur
Then all at once in that twilight gloom
Into the darkness they did zoom

Who he was I soon discovered
From her lure he had recovered
With no malice, he was actually pleased
My interest in her could be his release

Like a romance novel character
I promised I'd take good care of her
Now many years have passed in raptured glory
And it's only now that I can tell this story

I would do it all over and regret it not
This love affair has grown so hot
And by now you have guessed I'll bet
I just was talking about my Black Corvette

We Aim To Please
By George J. Kimble

Cars malfunction. It is well known
On occasion we realize something has blown
We think about the repair bill and mumble and groan
We then go to the repair shop "The Ludicrous Zone"
Do Do do do, Do Do do do

You limp your car in with a small odd noise
The service manager is younger than any of your boys
He writes down everything you say about your toy
Your worried look seems to give him joy
Do Do do do, Do Do do do

He is told it is just a little tic tic
You ask if he can fix it quick
His canned response is: after some diagnostics
He nods ominously to a sinister mechanic
Do Do do do, Do Do do do

You try to indicate it is in the front end
You try to emulate the sound and pretend
The manager calls over the wrench and two of his friends
You realize you are a sideshow and bring it to an end
Do Do do do, Do Do do do

Now suddenly appears some zombie looking man
He has carpet covers and plastic bags in his hand
He walks past three times where you stand
"All this to protect your car, Ain't it grand?"
Do Do do do, Do Do do do

He places the covers on the passenger's seat
He is careful and exceptionally neat
But that little performance will have no repeat
As he jumps right into the driver's side with his greasy feet
Do Do do do, Do Do do do

Now you are directed to the customer lounge
"Free coffee in there", for you to scrounge
You had a friend go in there and has never been found
You elect to tour the showroom and walk around
Do Do do do, Do Do do do

You wear out a new pair of shoes
Every sales person tries to sell something to you
You expected that, It is like paying your dues
But, You dispatch them all, just singing the blues
Do Do do do, Do Do do do

You hear your name over the P-A
You think, Boy, I'm out of here quick today!
You chase down the manager to hear him say
This is expensive, but luckily the part is on the way
Do Do do do, Do Do do do

This is when something strange attacks your brain
The time you ask him to please explain
He starts talking, but it is not very plain
He says, "It's the cross-over kinda-widget drain"
Do Do do do, Do Do do do

You say you have never heard of such a device
And how could it have such an awful price
"Okay" he says, "I'll be nice"
"The cost for labor, I will slice"
Do Do do do, Do Do do do

You will go home and wait, that is the plan
So now you walk to the courtesy van
Then you realize you walked, but you should have ran
Because, it is packed full, as a sardine can
Do Do do do, Do Do do do

You go to the waiting room filled with dread
So many bodies they all appear dead
Glazed eyes cast upon you, but nothing is said
You eye the clock and slowly shake your head
Do Do do do, Do Do do do

Seasons pass faster than a repairman's chore
Eternity will pass and Ravens speak nevermore
Before you are ever summoned through the door
To take that walk across the service bay floor
Do Do do do, Do Do do do

Now at last they say they are done
You write a check and that's no fun
You are given your keys at the setting of the sun
Now you experience the first test run
Do Do do do, Do Do do do

You head out toward your home
In a repaired car you start to roam
And when that damn Tic Tic starts to drone
You decide to fix it yourself and avoid, "The Ludicrous Zone"
Do Do do do, Do Do do do

Shade Tree
By George J. Kimble

Time comes and time goes
What's to come, no one knows
Changes happen for reasons that boggle the mind
Nowadays, mechanical systems have computers, of every kind
Cars, nowadays, are designed by a computer's plan
And the assembly lines, by Robots, are manned
In our cars the world has gone hyper-tech
It is for the environment and to reduce our ability to wreck
Computers measure the air to fuel mix
They make hydraulic brakes do non-slip tricks
Information about driver in-puts by Giga-bites
Determine if the driver is doing all right
Calculations in nano-seconds stream into cyber-brains
All this for better stops whenever it rains
Pitch and yaw get measured and to chips are dumped
Shocks are adjusted so our asses don't feel the bumps
Steering angle is delivered via fly by wire
No feel of the road does it require
Heads up displays blur the window screens
Flashing computer lingo; I don't know what it means
The computer keeps thieves from pilfering my glove box
When I leave my car it automatically locks
If perchance, the window, a crook breaks
Obscene sounds the computer makes
Headlights burn all day, to let others know, they are not alone
And I can take care of business on the installed cell phone
Laser and infra-red beams
Through fiber optic cable streams
Thousands of watts of audio power
Playing electronic music by the hour
If I am lost; Just push a button to satellite navigate
All these wonders are made so I can concentrate
When a nail makes a tire go flat
Detectors warn us all about that
But, we don't need to ever stop
Because, our run flats never go floppity-flop
Gee whiz and golly wow
What if I should hit a cow

Not to worry if you should have a crash
An air bag pillow is deployed from the dash
And to protect our precious bones
These machines have built in crumple zones
Engines dive to the ground
Just more pieces to be found
In time, we know, all things deteriorate
So at that time, we will commiserate
Lamenting, the Techno-mechanic's computer generated fee
And the days we did repairs under a big **Shade Tree**

CHAPTER TWO - History of Corvettes

Classic Glass	(Corvette History)	- 23 -
Instincts Of The Breed	(First NCM Caravan Experience)	- 25 -
Number Five Alive	(C-5 Is Produced)	- 27 -
Beyond Time	(Fifth Anniversary Caravan)	- 30 -
Who Was That Dreamer	(Salute To The Corvette Father)	- 32 -

Classic Glass
By George J. Kimble

The General decided to make a sports car
He wanted a two seater for a shining star
'53 was the beginning time
He didn't want owners to need a gold mine
He made it out of glass

He showed it off, an American dream?
Such a vehicle the people had never seen
A mighty blue flame six would power this
For the average guy to drive in bliss
He made it out of glass

Never before was there such a sleek design
All the young at heart for this car would pine
America was used to cars with lots of steel
Even racers wanted to get behind its wheel
He made it out of glass

Any man could afford a corvette on his wage
Chevy could now build upon a sporty image
Europe was the only place to build roadsters
"It just won't last", said all the big boasters
He made out of glass

Now forty odd years have come and passed
On many tracks the Ferraris and Porches were harassed
A good idea was sure to stick
Steady improvements was the trick
He made it out of glass

Duntov and others knew of course
Even a blue oval named after a horse
Could never steal this one's thunder
This little car was no blunder
He made it out of glass

He knew that in evolution
Around the tracks in many revolutions
He had to make it the fittest
He made changes to be the winningest
He made it out of glass

Now many have tried
And some came close
But most have died
And are now just ghosts
Corvette is the classic glass

Instincts of the Breed
By George J. Kimble

All along you had to know
This icon of yours had to go
The others would gather like a flock
From every city from every block
Like the horde they would rumble out

Over time you saw the wear
Here a chip and a scratch there
Change is certain for machine and man
Age is a wonder, time has no plan
You have changed, you have no doubt

But off a distant siren calls
A yearning to return beckons all
Though we are tattered and frail
Long and winding we retrace the early trail
"A sojourn starts with just one step," you shout

Buffed and pumped our tanks are full
In gilded armor to the muster we feel the pull
Others now a circling lot
Our leader's eyed, he's made his plot
Nervous thoughts as you ponder the long route

Like steeds of yore a caravan
We carefully follow our leaders plan
Horsepower strains at metal and glass
Upon the road we wheel at last
Shakes and rattles are a part of age's pout

Homecoming, what is that?
Old memories turned to fact?
Steady hands your youth did mold
To make you strong to make you bold
Every effort to render your clout

Upon arrival, many in your class
Have more gracefully weathered the past
Sheltered from the hourglass sands?
Restored by deft caring hands?
One's value is not easily seen from without

In front of the Museum, an honored post
Thousands of pilgrims from coast to coast
On every face a glorious smile
The long trek to Bowling Green was worth every mile
Our collective heart holds dear what it was all about.

Number Five Alive
By George J. Kimble

Riding along in my automobile
My baby is beside me; I'm behind the wheel
Rumbling along at sixty-two
A guy on the radio is crooning the blues

When suddenly in the lane on the right
My eyes behold a beautiful sight
There is a Stingray of shinning glass
Thundering engine slipping past

I get excited, filled with glee
And the Stingray guy waves back at me
I am a Corvette fan as my friends all know
I take my Corvette to all the shows

I tuck in behind him and try to settle down
We take the exit ramp to some little town
A big discount store I won't mention
A parking lot of ludicrous dimension

"Wholly Mackerel!" I shout out loud
I am stunned by the size of the crowd
C5's, late models, Rays and Sharks,
Straight axles, modifieds and GS's with red hash marks

This lot is filled with Corvettes all sparkling bright
Never before have I seen such a magnificent sight
Like fish shimmering in a trawler's net
It's a sparkling mass of Corvettes

It is still early, just past dark
I ease up slowly and shift my Corvette into park
I get out of my Corvette, looking pretty stupid
Like I am struck by an arrow from Cupid

I holler, "What's going on?" to one young man,
He yells back, "We're all part of The Caravan"
"The Nashville stop is our next to last,
"The final stop is The NCM's 5th Birthday Bash"

I tell my wife, "This looks like fun"
"I think I am going to join this run"
I sign some papers and some folks I greet
And quickly, this parade takes to the street

We arrive in Nashville around a quarter past eleven
"Look! Everywhere Corvettes! This must be heaven!"
Hundreds, No, thousands are circling Opryland
Then, I am told of everything that's been planned

As night shadows slowly begin to fall
We amble to the Corvette Lover's Ball
This is a happening. We just had to attend
Corvette pilgrims, fill the Delta Ballroom, end to end

There is food and drinks, and a cute little girl
She is belting out country songs, to the Corvette world
I eat, I dance, I mix and mingle
The excitement and enthusiasm makes me tingle

I meet and greet and shake so many hands
And talk and talk about the greatest car in the land
In the morning there is a call to re-assemble
At, Oh too early, we have to scramble

Disciples of fiberglass from across the planet
To this point, are drawn, as if to a magnet
I slurp hot coffee and a bagel, that is provided
The cars line up in rows, very evenly divided

A flash of blue light and a siren wails
Corvettes are in motion, nose to tail
We pull onto the highway called I-65
To Bowling Green, Kentucky, it's just a short drive

As far as I can see with my naked eye
A line of Corvettes under the bright morning sky
Corvettes in front and Corvettes behind
This moment forever imprinted upon my mind

On the way, slowly winding north
Great throngs of people have come forth
They wave and cheer, and many take photos
Their homage and respect paid our unique autos

But just as that thought rattled across my mind
We encounter more Corvettes from the North in a line
Now like two sea serpents off the interstate we wind
And onto Corvette Drive two long Caravans are combined

This experience assures all, it's great to be alive
An unprecedented salute to the Corvettes we drive
We are lucky the National Corvette Museum has survived
To grow from an idea, to celebrate "Birthday Number Five"

Beyond Time
By George J. Kimble

I was the essence of a nation emerging from a war
I was the heartbeat pounding from shore to shore
I met every challenge as I went about my chores
I still survive
I'm still alive

I was determination, purpose and solution
I was there in '53 summoned from a notion
I condensed within a form providing it with motion
I'm still alive
I still survive

I humiliated exotic invaders from every distant shore
I silenced the domestic forces who would steal my royal court
I laid waste to many foes confronted in my sport
I still survive
I'm still alive

I rode to heraldic glory with many men so proud
I prevailed in spectacles viewed by massive crowds
My name was often cursed in foreign voices loud
I'm still alive
I still survive

Through the decades I never really changed
I once grew very muscular and nearly lost my name
There was a time I lost my breath and suffered growing pains
I still survive
I'm still alive

Through all my regenerations I've heard them rant and rave
Many times esteemed pundits anointed me a grave
Too often now, from my chest, I've pulled their pointed stave
I'm still alive
I still survive

In my present form I appear very sleek
Though my body is growing old, don't assume I'm weak
Yet another transformation soon I'll surely seek
I still survive
I'm still alive

My future holds fulfillment of vast expectations
I will impress my will upon another generation
I shall be even bolder in my next incarnation
I will be alive
I will survive
I will be the motive force of the new Corvette "C-5"

Who Was That Dreamer?
By George J. Kimble

Automotive engineering was his dream
He wanted to be on a car design team
Facts , figures, inches and degrees
To him were not a mortal disease
He wanted to build the best racing machine

All his friends said ,"You'll never succeed"
"You think too much of engines and speed"
In a shed near a tall lone pine
He worked up a performance design
His heads made engines more powerful indeed!

Then with his heads and some good hearty mates
He campaigned his design throughout the States
In many races he did compete
His design was hard to beat
Here was a man that was destined to be great

His skills as an engineer became well known
At competitive racing he stood out alone
GM invited him in one day
They offered him a little pay
They turned over a project, that he took as his own

They wanted to inspire America's young men
To really get their hearts beating again
They wanted a super sports car
To hold up like a bright shining star
That could compete against the Europeans and win

From a shop with only some cryptic initials
He teamed up with a guy named Bill Mitchell
Though he had some factory help
The overall effort would be by himself
Then into speed contests and races he whistled

His cars often became tattered and torn
But for his efforts there never was scorn
One design then another
Labors of love like a brother
Out of his work the Sting Ray was born

Then one night right out of the dark
He dreamed up the famous Mako Shark
What a man, what a story
Lots of work, led to glory
And on our Corvettes he left his mark!

    SALUTE:
    Zora Arkus-Duntov 1909 – 1996

CHAPTER THREE - A Saga

Spirit of a Glass Horse	(Willie's Story)	- 35 -
Closing Time	(Angelina's Dream of Willie)	- 38 -
Unlikely Duet	(Roadhouse Encounter)	- 40 -
White Knuckled	(Willie and Angelina Chase)	- 43 -
Bad Mood Rising	(Playboy Attacks)	- 46 -
How Long Is Forever?	(Willie and Angelina Decision)	- 48 -

Spirit of a Glass Horse
By George J. Kimble

They called him Sweet Willie
He hailed from South Philly
His looks were as sharp as a stiletto knife
He rode the streets and lived the high life

His ride was a Sting Ray silver and sleek
All the young ladies, inside wanted to peek
The machine's clear coat looked like a million
On the hood was painted a prancing Stallion

He speaks with a sharp wit and tells his story
He leans and gestures weaving a tale of glory
He was born poorer than soil in the junkyard
He tells of a mother who always worked much too hard

He tells about the struggles to become a man
Of no father to lend him a hand
The frustration of schools with no understanding
The street wars over turf, so demanding

About hanging on street corners just killing time
Of a youthful lifestyle of petty crime
A listing of schemes, that always failed
Then a brief residency in an upstate county jail

He was out there once robbing a man's truck
He had sunk that low to make a buck
He was caught with his hands on the wheel
But the owner offered to make him a deal

The old owner called him a wayward youth
"You need to be shown the path of truth"
"You also have a mechanical knack"
"Now, get out of here, and in the morning come back"

Willie's release left him dumbfounded, surely
Willie showed up in the morning bright and early
The old man took him to an old warehouse
It was very shabby, unfit for a mouse

He slid open a massive wooden door
Revealing a dusty concrete floor
There were crates and boxes, cobwebs and dust
Car parts and motors covered with rust

"From here you'll find, a living can be made"
"If you are interested, I'll teach you my trade"
"I warn you Willie, nothing good comes easy"
"Now clean this place up, get yourself busy"

Willie looked deep into the old man's face
Around his eyes, wrinkles deeply traced
At first, Willie was indignant, angry and disgusted
A work detail, cleaning up, for getting busted

As he labored, the old man softly spoke
He remembered when car wheels had wooden spokes
He told of the Model A's and then the T's
After the war nobody wanted any of these

All the young men wanted modern steel
With long hoods and fins and shining wheels
With V-8's, overhead valves, and automatic transmissions
But he was more inclined to the European traditions

He liked sports cars, two seaters with styling
MG's and Triumphs and Healeys, got him smiling
His favorite was the Ferrari, the Prancing Horse
Expressing, the spirit of the man who built them, of course

Now, Willie came back day after day
He took to liking the old man, in a way
He was clever and could spin a great story
Wonderful tales of character and glory

He was amazed at the people the old man admired
Of hearing those stories he never tired
Willie was taught principles and every automotive part
He was absorbing it and taking it to heart

He learned tune-ups, oil changes and lubes
He was instructed in welding and forming of steel tubes
He started earning some money, but not a whole lot
He was in business; the old man had given him a shot

Willie worked hard and followed the old man's advice
"Treat your customers with respect and a fair price"
This business took off like a skyrocket
Soon he had money stuffed in every pocket

Willie returned to the shop very late each night
Building a sports car, in a corner out of sight
He owed the mentor his life and esteem
He was making, for him, a magnificent machine

He worried for weeks over the painting on the hood
He just hoped his adopted father would think it was good
He dreamed of the old man behind the wheel for a ride
The old man bestowed Willie his talents and essence of pride

But before Willie could give him this Silver Sting Ray
The old man had a an illness and passed away
Willie will let no one sit in, or get near it
Because in this Glass Horse rides the old man's spirit

Closing Time
By George J. Kimble

She has raven hair and eyes dark as coal
She has a sensuality that moves a man's soul
Angelina is her name and that fits her just so
She is an earthy expression with a celestial glow

She murmurs an enchanting melody as she works
Slowly swaying to the sounds as coffee perks
Her café customers enjoy the lilting tune
Secretly, she hopes Willie will come in soon

Willie is her customer for coffee everyday
He owns the auto shop across the way
He makes her feel like an innocent child
His looks and manners stimulate something wild

In this forgotten nook of the city, he is fresh air
Each night as he leaves, she enters a trance-like stare
Through her shop window, as she pulls the blinds
Fantasies, of rides in his Corvette, possess her mind

She has heard Willie's story of course
All about the Old Man and the Prancing Horse
She imagines, Willie and her, in that silver machine, top laid low
Cruising the warm evening, tenderly slow

As if real, she taste the warm night air
City lights glistening in his jet-black hair
His strong hands caress the Corvette's wheel
She envies that object's feel

Masculinity in his arms and chest are defined
The rumble of the engine is so sublime
Uncontrollable impulses of jealousy towards the leather seat
Holding his body and feeling it's heat

Tiny tremors of delight imperceptible
Overtake her body in the accelerating convertible
Primal urges straining to be understood
Like that stallion on the Corvette's hood

Her cheeks acquire a hue of rose
As if buffeted by the wind as it blows
Rushes of grand proportion keep building and building
Every night she has this dream so thrilling

So, thinly veiled, her emotion and desire
It is like the engine's internal fire
Everyone knows it is the source of the Corvette's power
Everyone knows she dreams of Willie hour by hour

This man and his Corvette are more than meets the eye
This woman and her emotions, descriptions defy
Her secret fantasies she cannot give away
So, she lets on he is just a customer by light of day

Unlikely Duet
By George J. Kimble

Outside the City limits the Roadhouse hung
Large gravel parking lot, Choppers and rods disorderly strung
Front porch with crates and empty kegs for stools
Occupied by tattooed, leathered variants of the gene pool

Now, ordinary citizens pass by here night after night
Probably making comments about this terrible blight
Discussing how something ought to be done
And that they've heard these people carry guns

Loud music blasting from behind neon beer signs
Even louder voices and laughter blurt out from time to time
Raven haired woman leans against a pillar and sings
Mouthing words in sync with music by Sting

A man with five o'clock shadow and sleeveless T-shirt
Wraps his arm around the waist of her mini-skirt
She shrugs and pushes him away
It's crystally apparent she doesn't want to play

Thin crescent sliver of a moon
Gives no luminance to the hot August gloom
Then gravel crackles and pops
A silver Corvette wheels in and stops

A lone male rider with long black hair
Hops over the closed convertible door and inhales the night air
It's a Corvette, wax and polish heavily applied
There are splatters and splashes of mud on either side

Two arches of dirt cover the windshield
It's no tractor, but it has been in the field
A sense of uneasiness among the Roadhouse group
This Corvette driver is not one of the Roadhouse troop

He walks with a swagger and disconcerting sway
The singer stares at him but her Playboy pulls her away
Playboy curls his lip in a defiant sneer
Everyone else side steps as the Vette driver walks near

At the passage into the bar room
He smells stale beer and cheap perfume
The jukebox stops with a clunk
Unplugged by a clowning drunk

The joint is silent as he approaches the bar
The barkeeper's face has a hideous scar
He hears a scream from behind his back
Playboy has given the singer a smack

Suddenly, that chick bolts through the door
Pursued by Playboy and slammed to the floor
The commotion rouses the patrons to cheers
Her face is bleeding and she is shedding tears

The Vette driver grabs her hand
He pulls her to his side and takes a stand
Silence fills the room, like fog on the moor
Playboy screams, "Get out of my way, I'm going to kill the whore"

Vette driver looks like the entrée in a wolf pack's meal
He knows the danger and he knows it's real
He stands pat, with no bluff in his eye
He whispers, "That's something you don't want to try"

There is a glint of steel, cold and blue
A flurry of bodies in motion ensues
A snarl, a scream, and a deafening thud
Playboy's body on the floor oozing blood

It happened so quick the crowd is dismayed
Some one yells, "Hey! Don't let them get away"
The girl and her hero fly towards the street
Then leap the doors into the Corvette seats

The starter engages and the engine roars
Tires spit gravel, onto the highway the Corvette soars
Bikers and Rodders run to their steeds
Abandoning Playboy on the floor to just bleed

Into the darkness they chased the Corvette
They never caught him, that's a sure bet
That night a duet was forged from considerable strife
I heard last week, Angelina and Willie may soon be husband and wife

White Knuckled
By George J. Kimble

You know they slipped away
To love and exist another day
But in the distance a rumbling sound
An omen as their Corvette rolls out of town

Like thunder beyond the horizon's view
A menacing hint of the impending havoc due
Spats of light pierce the windshield's glare
Jagged glints fill the midnight's air

Silhouettes of darting figures fill the mirror's sight
Marauders from hell, on iron steeds, corrupt the night
Leather clad and chromium draped, smoldering beast
A Horde, descending upon innocent prey, to feast

The riders in motion lean and sway
Headlights swirling across the passageway
Circling, road pirates, wailing epithets licentious
Closing in on the Corvette, with anger from the dark abyss

Angelina's face belies her apprehension
Terror is painted upon her like an artist's illustration
Her fists clench and she wets her quivering lips in nervous tension
Contemplation, anticipation, choked back fear of extinction

Calmly Willie grips his wheel
He portrays a man with nerves of steel
His concern is not loss of wealth
Nor is it even for himself

He plots a course in his mind
To disarm the pirates for all time
Steady pressure upon the machine's controls
Leave behind these nightmare shoals

Consequences of such endeavors
Often reveals them not so clever
Speed is a dangerous friend
It has been known to abruptly end

Racing the goons from their roadhouse lair
Seems a challenge for the mentally impaired
But this is a Corvette with ample horsepower in it
And this is the life and death decision minute

This road beyond the tracks
Is as treacherous as a snake in a sack
Signs advise caution, to take special care
Curves, switchbacks, esses everywhere

Through this gauntlet over a rise
Around a cliff and mountain side
The bandits and Corvette fly
Motorcycle and Corvette side by side

Just one face of awful craze
Of one rider, the moonlight betrays
The sneering scar of the bartender's features
The leader of these hideous creatures

Willie taunts these animals with controlled aplomb
He is sure they are vicious and also dumb
He knows this road like the back of his hand
He will use it to send these mongrels to the Promised Land

Faster and faster he speeds into the obscurity
Head long into the night he plunges for Angelina's security
Breakneck Corvette careening
Gravity defying motorcycles leaning

Defeated Creek Bridge, rapidly looming
One way passage, hard into 90 zooming
Tires howling, engines roaring, lights flashing
Cycles crashing, metal crushing, men screaming, Corvette leaving

Willie looks at Angelina with confidence in his eye
Angelina now breaks into a full-throated cry
She grasps his shoulder and sobs
He has disposed of the heathen slobs

Their lives to the precipice were thrust
On his Corvette and skill he laid uncommon trust
There will grow upon this foundation
The fruit of this uncommon relation

Bad Mood Rising
By George J. Kimble

What brought this sweet girl to a place like this?
Was it the danger, or the promise of a hard kiss?
A promise, of honest money for her talented voice?
Whatever, it was, It was a bad choice

The Playboy with a special agenda of his own
Enticed her there completely alone
Her Cafe's mortgage was way past due
Sometimes a Girl has to do, what a Girl has to do

The Playboy's offer of employment was accepted
The job singing was with out strings connected
The playboy's problem; his advances were rejected
The poor fool felt down right neglected

Then his behavior was less than Chivalrous
He wound up beaten and delirious
Angelina escaped that night at Willie's side
That night, they took the wild Corvette ride

Suddenly Playboy appears in the cafe's neighborhood
Angelina knows; he is up to no damn good
It is late, way after dark
She's watching Willie, while he tunes up a Shark

Playboy appears in the shadows wielding a club
Stealing ever closer behind the landscaping shrubs
Angelina's heart drops to the floor
As she bolts to the Café door

She grabs the nearest thing to use as a weapon
A 14-inch skillet as she runs through the kitchen
Her voice is like a siren loudly screaming
Down her cheeks, tears are abundantly streaming

Playboy is moving like a Leopard in the night
Angelina has focused on him in the dim light
His advance is arrested as she strikes with the pan
The skillet to the head brings down the dangerous man

She pushes him aside with a bellow of power
She is the Valiant, the woman of the hour
Willie was shocked by her control and determination
For her, he was filled with nothing but admiration

To calm her, he offers a smile
Then calls the police, after awhile
Now Playboy, for some time, will be gone
Angelina sings softly and Willie hums along

I relayed this legend of urban life in many of verse
Your time spent reading could have been spent worse
Ever after and for a long time now
These two souls and a Corvette remain tied together somehow

How Long Is Forever?
By George J. Kimble

Willie admired Angelina, on at least one occasion,
She had saved his bacon
He was a car nut, and for business that was good
Angelina was frustrated because he was always under a car hood

Angelina wanted to see Willie alone
She wished to know him with out the stresses they had known
She invited him to share a meal
She needs to tell him just how she feels

Willie accepted her invitation
His ego suffered from dramatic inflation
She, to him, was a statue of carved art
She had won over his vulnerable heart

Willie washed and waxed the Glass Horse Corvette
He reserved a table for two at this town's best
If his friends knew, they would surely die
He even put on a silken necktie

To Angelina's street Willie rode
There were flashing lights ablaze at her abode
His heart raced with alarm
His muscles twitched in his arm

He prayed she was okay
This was to be their most important day
Tears uncontrollably rolled down his face
As he remembered Angelina's warm embrace

Willie leaped from the Vette, His face covered with concern
He questioned by-standers but nothing could be learned
The perimeter of men, dressed in blue
Restraining him, offered no clue

The entrance with yellow tape was blocked
Her neighbors stood around in a state of shock
They said, "Sometime earlier in that day",
"Angelina had left her little Café"

"From the café to the bank she had walked,
To one shopkeeper she had politely talked"
"All the while a villain secretly stalked"
"And now on her carpet a body's outline was chalked"

"Two shots were fired", several folks had heard,
"Who was shooting and who was hit? There wasn't any word"
Willie was overcome by anger and pain
He had to get answers to settle his brain

Finally, through the police barricade he broke
Then to a razor faced detective he spoke
A man who eyed him like a bird eyes a worm,
Every question Willie uttered the detective, weighed and turned

He was an inspector of homicide
There were forensic people busy inside
Willie asked, "What happened, had she been raped?"
"Had that jerk, Playboy, from jail escaped?"

The detective told Willie, "Be calm and relax"
"Angelina was fine, She stopped Playboy forever, dead in his tracks"
"Playboy was the one outlined on the floor,
She had shot him with a Colt forty-four"

"She had answered all their questions and they were satisfied"
"This punk did wrong and for that, he had died"
"He could talk to her now, if he pleased"
When he saw her, Willie dropped to his knees

From his pocket, he pulled a small diamond ring
He asked her to marry him and make him feel like a king
She accepted his offer forever, and held him close to her breast
Their love again had survived a furious test

You know how Angelina and Willie came together
And how they came through some pretty stormy weather
This is the story of how their world became so much better
And how Willie proposed to wed her forever.

The lives of some are easy to render
The lives of others are destined to surrender
Each of us has only one life to live
The question is: What are we willing to give?

These two are better now because they will never be alone
They will soon have children and make them a home
Forever is a very long time
And now finally, I have finished this rhyme

CHAPTER FOUR – Stranger Than Fiction

Ah!	(Corvette Experienced)	- 52 -
Another Dimension	(Corvette Acts as Time Machine)	- 53 -
Destiny	(Strange End in a Corvette)	- 54 -
Speed Demons	(A Really Bad Dream)	- 56 -
Jagged Edge	(Wrong Exit)	- 58 -

Ah!
By George J. Kimble

Ah, the symbiosis,
Mechanized thrombosis,
Human narcosis,
Spring's delight

Ah, the acceleration,
The exhilaration,
The integration,
Man and machine

Ah, the engineering,
The steering,
The appearing,
Kinetic energy

Ah, the dials,
The miles,
The smiles,
Exquisite harmony

Ah, The stratagem,
No boredom,
The freedom,
Cosmic relief

Ah, the power,
The passing of hours,
The complimentary showers,
Corvette experienced

Another Dimension
By George J. Kimble

Time and space
Contemplate
Undulating black ribbon
White lines hypnotized
Corvette driven aimlessly
Kamikaze insects on windshields
What of their fate?
Ideas wash in and fade
Ephemeral tides in the twilight mind's eye
Wheels eerily chant
Octet of muffled voices reverberate from hooded chamber
Baroque images conjured
Moon shadows cast by barren trees
Black flames cascaded upon still life surfaces
Static crackles upon distant airwaves
Hounds bay in fallow barnyards
Rusting hulk implement of tillage
Autumn's melancholy breath wafts,
Burnt leaves pungent scent
Aroused ancient savoring of that first sighted,
Corvette
Gray mantled being
Physical prowess feebled
Keenness undiminished
Common places experienced
Transcendental, Hyper-dimensional
Never routine
Corvette is the ultimate time Machine

Destiny
By George J. Kimble

Wiping eyes filled with residue of the Sandman's endeavors,
Hot Java essence inhaled, oblivious to karma.
Sunrise still a fleeting thought to the darkness of the night.
The Corvette quivers as if shaking off a chill.
The gut emptying sound of steel engaging steel,
Fluids wend through once dormant courses and feed flames of muted pulse.
Creeks, groans and coughs of awareness forthcoming.
Then growl of aroused archaic canine primordials.
Gravel clawing gravel, under pressurized rolling Gatorbacks,
Beams of yellow split the silent gloom, searching the slope to the macadam below.
Slipping, like an eel, onto the darkened stream, of white delineated undulating desert byway.
Resonance of four black choir members humming in ever increasing a cappella harmony,
Howl of speed induced dense air leaking through invisible crannies, annoying,
Reassuring, there is another sense responding to the surreal environs so encompassed.
Eastward trek, racing the gathering dawn to the distant horizon.
No other soul is destined to wander the abandoned landscape
The Corvette slinks onward.
Distant repetitions of mindless signals,
Conditioned, by daytime habits, conducting fleets of wandering ants.
Ignored!
Above, tailed by contrails unseen in the moonless ether,
Some camouflaged transporter of massive proportion,
Flies laden, with residue hauling enclosed tanker.
Some newly developed panacide to frighten all who would threaten.
Some latch forgotten on clasp and bond releases,
And aloft motion begot wheels untethered.
Hurled, acceleration enhanced by gravity's lure to the central core.
A glint in the pinking sky.
The Corvette driver contemplates the object of his demise.
Smashing, blinding, splintering.
No one heard!
Reports are written and indictments follow,

"A careless driver failed to yield and fate was served upon his flesh."
Surely, he was ignorant of the signal at the crossway.
Yet as one evaluates destiny, no one can escape,
Alert or dim, none can select the time, nor give a reason, for the Reaper's Harvest.
Though ends are, alas, inevitable, never anticipated,
Go forth, into the unlit future, each Earthly second appreciated.

Speed Demons
By George J. Kimble

It came to me last night in a dream
A hazy discontent through mist and steam
An automobile surrounded by ghosts
A sticklike man speaking as the host

The car was smoldering and all aglow
The ghosts were hovering above and below
Some wore gloves and helmets adorned their heads
I realized these were the spirits of drivers long dead

I queried the phantoms about their presence
In one voice, they extolled their essence
"We are the spirit of the machine; present and past"
"We invite you to our realm, the Dominion of Go Fast"

Being a man of substance, I wasn't too scared
I have been known to go fast, whenever I'm dared
As if weightless, into the cockpit my body fluttered
I tried to scream but no sound was uttered

The auto was a roadster, of that, I was sure
But the design was something extraordinarily pure
Its parts were all from different models and makes
Each piece expertly crafted without any mistakes

The gauges shown white, like a pretty girl's teeth
I surmised the dials were illuminated from beneath
The controls were fitted with leather as tight as a thief's glove
The seats were as comfortable as an old couple's love

The body was voluptuous with curves sublime
A sculpture of zoom, transcending time
From within the hood, an exalting purr
Like a lion's voice, when licking his fur

I heard exhaust tones, deep and melodic
The maiden's song, completely hypnotic
Now, the ephemeral ones set it all into action
And smiled with cruel satisfaction

I gripped the wheel with focused resolution
I was in a speed trap with no solution
My sleeping brain was filled with confusion
I could not awaken, from this terrible illusion

The machine seemed unwaveringly firm
As if we were planted and the whole earth turned
I eyed the approaching horizon with sober concern
A cliff was approaching, with no where to turn

Over the precipice, bolting autos burst into flame
Like playing a movie, frame by frame
Closer and closer the fear in me is mounting
In the distance a haunting voice is counting

To the edge and over; I am falling
A loud voice, my name is continuously calling
Headlong, plummeting, a white blur, of light in my brain
The excitement was more than a dream can contain

Upright I bolt, in my bed
I pinch myself to assure I'm not dead
This weird scene, now replays in my head
It was just a dream, nothing more needs to be said

Jagged Edge
By George J. Kimble

Jagged edge, where concrete marries steel
Vision unearthly, very surreal
Surfaces sweat, a rain unseen
Nervous tension, ultra keen
Labyrinth of potholes and broken glass
Stench of humanity, the unwashed mass
The wrong exit, from the well-beaten path
A caldron belching, the demons wrath
Street lamps glow, but shadow prevails
Through the gloom, a siren wails
Young men hanging, without a care
Their lost hope fills the air
Gauge warning of fuel ominously low
You brood over how far you can go
A well-lit gas station is what is needed
Your prayer for divine guidance goes unheeded
Should you stop and confront these men?
And try to coax from these dubious friends,
Some semblance of redirection
Or just proceed further, without detection
In this realm, the Corvette you drive
Does not enhance your ability to survive
As you pass through a tunnel unlit at the end
You weigh life's meaning again and again
In life, many off ramps lead to desolation
It's these times of tribulation
These digressions, from your dreamed destination
That humbles you to resignation
You drive your Corvette so cavalier
And over look those things, you should hold dear
Values are not made of fiberglass and steel
Nor are they rolled out on four wheels

And though each day may bring some strife
A good day is marked, by each breath of life
Because of nightmares you contemplate with dread
You are stronger because you are not dead
With poignantly depicted lives unraveled
You learned this, from the maze you traveled
With confidence and honest resolution
Attack life, as an adventure, with an unknown conclusion
Now reassured in your darkest hour
The road ahead, blooms like a Spring flower

CHAPTER FIVE – Fantasies

Hound And The Hare	(Night In The Desert)	- 61 -
110 In The Shade	(Penalty in Louisiana)	- 63 -
Heat Stroke	(Everything Changes)	- 66 -
Plan Brown Rapper	(Corvette Street Racer)	- 69 -
Primer Gray After Dark	(Viper Vs. Vette Drag)	- 71 -
Pumping Iron	(Found a Big Block)	- 73 -
Switcharoo	(Making A Ford Go Fast)	- 75 -
Reality Check	(The Perfect Road)	- 77 -
Vette Dreams	(Corvette Sensuality)	- 79 -

Hound and the Hare
By George J. Kimble

Out on that West Texas plain
A couple dozen miles out of Loraine
I had the Vette in cruise
Rolling like plain folks do

Late at night and growing weary
With patches of mist the desert is scary
No traffic out there to break the monotony
All alone and dreamy thoughts coming to me

When, there in the mirror
Something in the mist, was getting clearer
It was closing in fast
I was glad to have some company at last

It was a big Caddy Eldo
Flying wide and flying low
I thought, OK, you are the hare
I am the hound, as long as I dare

Figured if the man had tickets to write
I'd just keep that Eldo barely in sight
It wasn't my plan to go to jail!
I'll keep some distance as I trail

Roads in West Texas are straight and flat
Nothing but sagebrush and things like that
The Caddy was slipping out of view
I kept bumping up the cruise

Miles came and miles went
Caddy was booking, like a tenant that can't pay the rent
Faster and faster hour after hour
They build those Caddies with plenty of power

I guessed out here, there ain't no speed trap
And decided to close the gap
Took it out of cruise and grabbed fifth
Rounded a little curve in a four wheel drift

Pegged it and saw the back of the driver's head
Closed in, like the reaper on the dead
I pulled along side, the mist was a swirl
The Eldo was driven by a girl

I asked the Vette for just a little bit more
As I got even to her door
I could see her smile as she laid the hammer down
This was a hare that liked to tease the hound

Caddy and Vette neck to neck
Two-lane highway, what the heck
Off in the distance, a semi truck
How far could we push the luck?

Like two cats on an alley fence
Things were getting sort of tense
Was this a mistake?
Should I tap my brake?

Head lights getting too near
This rabbit had no apparent fear
High beams start to flash
I brake, let it pass

Next instant that lady is gone
Sky is lighted in the dawn
No Eldo, no tail lights
Strange things happen in the desert at night

I pull into a filling station
Get a cup of coffee, try to stop shaking
I tell my story to the locals there
They laugh, "I'm not the first hound to chase the phantom hare"

One Hundred And Ten in The Shade
By George J. Kimble

I was pushing across the bayou country of Louisiana
Tip toe crushing the gas pedal like a banana
My long hair tied back in a bright blue bandanna
The old Corvette Sting Ray is hauling me to see my sweet Rosy Anna

I must have been doing a shade over One Hundred and Ten
I was crossing one of those long wooden bridges with alligators under them
I hadn't seen a place to pull over since I don't know when
All of a sudden, cutting through the swamp vapors, I heard a siren

Wherever that Parish Constable was hid, I'll never know
He was whipping that old four door Pontiac as fast as it would go
His siren wailing, headlights blinking, and bubble gum machine all aglow
For a moment, I contemplated hammering it just to see that poncho blow

But instead, I just slowed down
And started looking to pull over onto some solid ground
And finally spotted a sandy mound
I can still hear that eerie siren sound

The sunglassed stereotypical constable stopped and jumped out
He didn't have a PA system and just began to shout
"Put your hands up and get your butt out!"
He had his pistol drawn and he meant business I had no doubt

He said, "Put both hands on the trunk of the car"
On his chest was pinned a brightly polished star
He grabbed one hand, then the other and cuffed them really hard
That angered me, but I knew better than to hassle that tub of lard

He was huffing and puffing and sweat formed on his brow
He spoke in a "Cajun" accent in a guttural growl
He yammered, "You gonna see the Judge now"
Then he dragged me back to that Pontiac scow

He turned the cruiser around in a blur
I asked, "What about my Corvette sir?"
He just acted as if he couldn't hear
And then asked if I'd been drinking beer

We pulled into a town built along a railroad track
There was a brick building surrounded by a lot of shacks
My hands were sore, cuffed behind my back
Moreover, this fine officer wasn't going cut me no slack

The judge appeared blind in one eye and couldn't see from the other
He was the spitting image of the cop, they must be brothers
I started saying my prayers to the holy mother
When I saw them whispering one to another

The proceedings were short and concise
For my indiscretion of speed, I would have to pay a price
Since I was sober, the judge would be nice
But, 110 meant the penalty would be compounded twice

The debt that now must be paid
Was sixty days of labor in these everglades
Clearing brush from the roadside with a machete blade
Every day has been at least 110 in the shade

I was treated worse than a new army recruit
I did my time in a striped suit
I was warned the guard would shoot
And had blood hounds in case of pursuit

They turned me loose after many appeals
And, when I asked about my wheels
They chuckled and laughed with little squeals
The giggled they had sold it to pay for my meals

Every one knows swamps are filled with scary creatures
We have seen them in late night movie features
But, I was never informed by my teachers
Nor enlightened in church by my preachers

About the predators who cast a net
Who upon a traveler are beset
That I encountered with regret
That devoured two months and my Red Corvette

Heat Stroke
By George J. Kimble

The heat, the dust
The course east across the desert crust
The miragic shimmer on the endless blacktop
The Corvette seats sticking to the back of my shirt top

I pushed on speeding with no remorse
I was on a mission, a survivor of divorce
She got the house, the mini van, and personal checks
But, she was not going to get, my old Corvette

The fuel gauge was sinking ominously low
The engine was hot and I feared it would blow
When I spotted the station, it seemed another mirage
But, soon I could read the rusty sign, "Desert Lodge"

We've all seen these arcane sites
Oasis overcome by years of blight
A dinner and hotel in combination
Just to the rear of the filling station

I pull in and create an awesome dust cloud
The sweat and dust make mud on my brow
As I stand, my head is all a whirl
The heat is stifling, I almost hurl

A three toothed old man in a dingy T-shirt
Walks up and ask, "Stranger are you hurt?"
"You look kind of ill"
"You had better just stand still"

I reply, that I am all right
But, that Sun seems excessively bright
He says, "Stranger you need a rest"
"I'll fill your tank with high test"

He moves in slow motion to start that chore
I stagger and stumble to the dinner door
Struggling, in the darkened dinner, to focus my eyes
I can smell the aroma of fresh baked pies

I plunk my butt on a red covered stool
There's an overhead fan blowing some cool
To my right, there's a box of ICE COLD POP
On another stool sits the local cop

He looks at me then out the window
He says, "That your Vette? How fast will it go?"
It's hard to talk when your mouth is so dry
But, I manage to mumble that it will fly

A beautiful woman, on the counter, sets some water
I grab it and guzzle, thinking she must be the owner's daughter
The cop lays down some change as he leaves
The swinging door kicks up a little breeze

The old man comes in and says," Your Vette is filled up son"
The lady says, "I love Corvettes, No one around here ever had one"
Her voice is light and extremely soothing
Very melodic, in her Southwestern drawling

The old man says, "I don't mean to be rude"
"But, I get paid for the gas, before you get your food"
Forty two fifty is his exorbitant price
I realize, it won't do any good to gripe

I tell the beauty I'm ready to eat
And ask, what goes good with all this heat?
She smiles and prepares a cold cuts platter
I can't help myself; I just keep staring at her

She says, "The deserts days are awfully hot"
But, "The nights really are not"
I eat the food very slow
Something is making me not want to go

We converse just to be polite
I ask her, how much it cost to spend the night?
She tells me and adds, she was once a bride
Unfortunately her young husband died

Casually she says, "If you stay the night,
You could take me for a ride, it would be a delight"
I almost choked on a chunk of meat
Then I realized she meant on the Corvette seat

I stayed and we took that Corvette ride
I'm ashamed; that I was glad her husband had died
I never thought to stay in the desert
And, I did buy "Pops" a new T-shirt

If it weren't for that Corvette
I wouldn't be so happy, you can bet
Stranger things could happen in life
But, I am glad I made that beauty my wife

Plain Brown Rapper
By George J. Kimble

Five Point Oh and my LT One
Mustang bumpin' bass like a gun

On a dark street side by side
Vette's already, gonna ride

Three hundred horses chompin' at the bit
Pony and Bow Tie just won't quit

Engines strainin' in the night
Hold the clutch wait for the light

> Street Racer, Crazy Greaser
> Call me what ya like
> Sounds bumpin', tires jumpin'
> Lets go racin' tonight

Smoke and nitro in the air
Money bet on a dare

Street racin' it ain't legal
Win the money, soar like an eagle

Dump the clutch, grab that gear
This is the time to have no fear

Street lights flashing, look like dots
Oh my God I think it's the cops

> Street Racer, Crazy Greaser
> Call me what ya like
> Sounds bumpin', tires jumpin'
> Let's go racin' tonight

Winnin's spent to go on bail
Ol' man found out. Kicked my tail

No new tires for my Vette
Gotta find a Mustang, make a bet

Turbo's screamin', sounds real bad
That Saleen Mustang can be had

All them Ponies wanna try,
But this LT One can really fly.

>Street Racer, Crazy Greaser
>Call me what ya like
>Sounds bumpin', tires jumpin'
>Let's go racin' tonight

Next time you're out late at night
Check the machines at the light

Every night again and again
On the streets, it's what's happenin'

Street racin' may be a crime
Put up your money, bet a dime

Dudes and dudettes hear my cry
I'll be runnin this Vette 'til I die

>Street Racer, Crazy Greaser
>Call me what ya like
>Sounds bumpin', tires jumpin'
>Let's go racin' tonight

Primer Gray After Dark
By George J. Kimble

He has grease under his fingernails
Levi's under his shirttails
He's got a creeper in his garage
He's working on a motor, rather large

He leans over low and sleek
And gives the ignition another tweak
The Vette wears primer and knock off wheels
To him it's not how it looks, but how it feels

His ideal ain't no beauty show
His ambition is grab it and go
He'll labor there for hours
Then onto the street, in lust for power

Crusin' past the drive-in
Local cops all think it's a sin
Sociabilty test? Probably failed.
Cops want to put him in jail

Mustang at the next red light
Those Pony drivers think they own the night
Mustang drivers never run for much
Most will only bet ten bucks

Viper slips out of it's lodge
Boy is that a steamin' Dodge
V-10 power and manual clutch
Would that challenge the Vette too much?

With a gesture from the hand
Viper pulls up to make a stand
The driver is smiling proud
Low side pipes growling loud

A short moment to set the prize
A long look into each other's eyes
Back at home mechanical parts
On the street a racer's heart

On the light his mind does rest
He's confident the Vette will stand the test
RPM's rising high
Dump the clutch; let it fly

He didn't build the Vette for turnin' corners
He's got it lit on all eight burners
Tires squat under torque
Grab a gear, feel the engine work

Eighth mile whizzes by
Vette is trailing by a wink of an eye
Viper needs to shift a gear
Vette grabs third, squall is all you hear

Quarter mile was just a flash
Shut it down, collect the cash
Get back home and check it out
Get it ready for tomorrow's bout

On the streets there's no checkered flag
On the street there's no time to brag
When he wins he feels real giddy
For his adversaries he has no pity

He may not be the local hero
But he knows he fastest starting from zero
If you think you can beat him
Come on out any night and meet him

Always waiting for another bet
Another challenge for his Vette
He'll be crusin' past your park
Primer Gray After Dark!

Pumping Iron
By George J. Kimble

He was a skinny looking kid
He couldn't do athletics like the others did
He always had sand kicked into his face
To his sisters he was a big disgrace

His shirt had pen marks over the pocket
His beady eyes were sunk deep within their sockets
He was comfortable with algebra books and beakers
Corduroy pants and black high topped sneakers

When he was sixteen he learned how to drive
He had saved all his money since he was age five
He set out alone to find himself some wheels
None of the tote the note lots would cut him a deal

While walking home, he spied a poster
FOR SALE, Chevrolet, by original owner
Exterior red, Interior black
Tires good, Paint inferior

The hand written sign seemed a little strange
He wrote down the number, it was a local exchange
In his house, he picked up the phone
It rang and rang as if no one was home

After several tries he heard, "Hello"
The voice of an old woman, soft and mellow
He quickly mentioned the hand lettered sign
Asked her address, she said, "South Main corner of Pine"

He asked many other questions, but received few replies
"Yes, It was old" a sixty something she surmised
"It had been setting so long it's battery was probably not alive"
"If he had an interest he should take it for a drive"

He begged his big sister to carry him there
She said, "Okay", as soon as she finished doing her hair
On the way, he bought new cables in a box
He went to the door and gave a great knock

He noticed a barn out in back
Then the door opened just a small crack
He heard that small voice coming from within
It said, "Go around back", where she would meet him

At the barn door, he gave his mightiest tug
With a second try, it finally budged
There were cobwebs and a great deal of clutter
In a finger of sunlight, he saw a figure under a cover

Coughing from dust in a cloud
Slowly he peeled back the shroud
With a terrible shiver, all up his spine
He beheld an Icon frozen in time

Her asking price was incredibly small
Since it was a Chevrolet Corvette side pipes and all
Since his good fortune and spectacular find
He has remained frail, gentle, and kind

Now, no one insults him and calls him an elf
He is simply referred to as:
MR. BIG BLOCK THE SOLID LIFTER HIMSELF

Switcharoo
By George J. Kimble

Ol' Billy was a proud man
He always polished his car
He'd buff and wax 'til every damn part was shinning like a mid-night star

The girl's name was Lucy
She really knew how to drive
She could grab those gears and could out shift any darn man alive

Now, Billy had an urgency
He liked to drive too fast
He had a big right foot and you know he kept it on the gas

One night Billy was out driving
He was trying to make a bet
That's when he was humiliated, by Lucy in her red Corvette

He had a bad, bad seven-liter Ford
The baddest machine in precinct or ward
Meanest car of it's kind
Faster than a bum, jumpin' on a dime

Now the two cars took to racin'
Rubbin' fenders and Bumpin' doors
Billy's foot slipped off the clutch and his tranny came through the floor

Lucy was a nice girl
She hated to see a grown man cry
She told him to go fix that Ford, and she'd give him another try

You Know Billy wasn't stupid
Some even called him wise
When he came back, that Ford, would be highly customized

Now, the time was a little later
Maybe, about a month or so
And Billy was begging Lucy, to have another go

He had a bad, bad seven-liter Ford
Baddest machine in precinct or ward
Meanest car of it's kind
Faster than a bum, jumpin' on a dime

This time things were different
Billy made no goofs
He out ran ol' Lucy, and I swear I'm telling the truth

Lucy didn't fall for that
But she was quite dismayed
She demanded to peek under his hood, before she would pay

Ol' Billy got very irritated
And that was her first clue
The big block was Chevy orange and not Ford dark blue

Lucy condemned Ol' Billy
You should be doing time
Because, to put a Chevy mill, inside a Ford, has got to be a crime

Billy had to soon confess
He cheated to win their bet
And his four door Ford was really an over-sized Corvette

He had a bad, bad Chevy powered Ford
Most modified machine in precinct or ward
Strangest car, one of a kind
Faster than a bum jumpin' on a dime

Reality Check
By George J. Kimble

Oh, How great a world it would be
For an old Corvetter just like me
To have a place on the open Highway,
To have that Super Slab my way

A road devoid of Mini vans
Cell phone users driving with both hands
No Semi's drearily lugging up hill
Winnebagoes corralled in parking lots still

A place, where ol' beater isn't driven by a drunk
No road kills, not even a dead skunk
All truck tires remaining on their rim
My hot coffee never spilling over the brim

No kamikaze bugs or fresh hot tar
Glistening paint and fresh tires on my car
Ticket givers asleep on the roadside
My best friend just along for the ride

Left lane loafers quickly pull to the right
No double bottom trailers are anywhere in sight
Every traffic light is permanently green
Gas station restrooms are immaculately clean

No glare of Sun beams into my eye
No insect in my cabin nor buzzing fly
At night, on coming lights are kindly muted
No horns blown or angrily tooted

Potholes have all been eliminated
Every off ramp is well illuminated
Easily seen directional signs
Traffic congestion is only behind

Road construction done only at night
No litter, trash, nor roadside blight
Speed limits are completely removed
Corvette tires sticking like they are glued

Other's, lane changes are always signaled
Once over, their flasher, is promptly canceled
Sunday drivers all stayed at home
Open highway for my Corvette to roam

With such a place, I know, no one is blessed
These crazy notions, I should arrest
My brain surgery, they say went well
And soon, they will release me from this padded cell

NO PARKING ON PAVEMENT

Vette Dreams
By George J. Kimble

She sees the man on the darkened street
The motor pulse matches her heart beat
He sees her and starts to grin
She likes the set of his squared chin

Confident and bright, their eyes meet
She motions him into the Corvette's seat
The engine growls low and deep
From the curb she starts to creep

He detects the scent of gas and nitrous
He thinks to himself, "this vette could be serious"
He smiles and asks, "How fast will it go ?"
She laughs and lies, "I really don't know."

Onto the street with a jerk of the wheel
She grabs second, the tires squeal
Deep down inside she loves the throb
The Corvette motor transmits to the shifter knob

He looks over to check on the tach
She hits third and the seat slaps his back
Around the bend and up the hill
Miles per hour climbing still

In fourth gear the Corvette engine roars
Like an airplane as it soars
Flying low across deserted land
She drives the Vette with the caress of her hand

Star light and Moon beams dance on the hood
The wind in her hair feels so good
He shouts "Girl you sure can drive!"
The Corvette makes her feel completely alive.

Reveling in a sense of power
They roll on hour after hour
Nerves and sinew and intense emotion
Perspiring brows, a beast in motion

She wets her lips and it evaporates
Over the hills they undulate
Abandoned thoughts and freedom's flight
Drinking up the essence of the night

He pinches himself, He must be dreaming
A beautiful woman and a Corvette screaming
Lust of speed at Corvette's full song
She does not stop 'til the crack of dawn

Winding down to the very last exit
A cup of coffee and another cigarette
With a sharp glance like cold blue steel
She is gone. Was she real?

CHAPTER SIX – Life Experienced

What Happened?	(Getting a Kids First Project)	- 82 -
Quest For The Bubble	(Finding a Special Part)	- 85 -
A Feeling Like This	(Broke Down On The Road)	- 88 -
Poof	(Thieves)	- 90 -
Lifted	(Saved By Angels)	- 93 -
To The Bone	(Snow Driving Experience)	- 96 –

What Happened?
By George J. Kimble

Me and the boy looking for that car
We had searched near and far
Everything we saw, he said, just was not up to par
It may be easier to reach out and touch a star?

Then we came upon that special one
He cried, "Pop this is going to be so much fun"
It was a Rust Bucket and wouldn't even run
There were holes in it, shot by a gun

That old coupe was anything but a find
To his eye it was a gem in his youthful mind
He saw magic in that paint that wouldn't shine
It looked like it soaked too long in a vat of brine

Youthful will stirs, youthful desires
Broken glass, shattered headlights, deflated tires
Sunk into the yard, totally mired
A love struck teenager, embraced by the one he admires

Talk all you want and the faults are never heard
Flap your lips and he never hears a word
Point out blemishes and he whistles like a bird
Your views, after the car, and his friend's opinions, are third

Then another tactic is tried,
Mom will be so mad, she will cry!
She will hang me out to dry!
Don't make me be the one to die!

You realize it to be natural truth
Big dreams are a fact of youth
Not even an inch will he move
He imagines himself in some kind of groove

He is struck
You are stuck
Go get the trailer and the truck
Hope you negotiate with better luck

Maybe you will lose
That may be a good excuse
To leave that heap in the junk yard ooze
Blame the owner for being so obtuse

The crusty, bearded, cigar chomping man didn't look too nice
However, He throws out a ridiculously low price
You cut it with a big sweeping slice
He accepts and you fall over, as if on Ice

Load that "beauty" onto the trailer you tell the boy
You mumble something about kids and toys
And the kinds of people Junk Yards employ
More over, you see your son jump for joy

On the trip you scold him. "You drag it home"
"You strip it to the bone"
"You do this on your own"
"You leave my tools alone"

The neighbors look in disgust at the beast
Their concerns are your least
That woman inside the house has to be appeased
You know she is not going to be easily pleased

Unloading you start a new lecture
Our subdivision is not a farmyard or a pasture
Do you realize this isn't a pretty picture?
This thing cannot become a backyard fixture

You look into his eyes and are amazed
His face is beaming and those eyes are glazed
The steering wheel is fixed in his immature gaze
By your discourse he has not been fazed

Wonders do sometimes thrust upon our lives
Sometimes they are stuck into our souls like knives
Suddenly, I relive the moment, when I learned to drive
I remembered how I had to beg and connive

Now, I too am magically blissed
Like the first time I was kissed
A feeling obscured by age, dearly missed
To my carefree youth I have been whisked

Kids and old cars are strange concoctions
Mixed in just the right proportions
They cross time and life's commotions
Evoking the most enjoyable emotions

As a man and a Dad
I will always become glad
Whenever I recall this time we had
And try to remember, that old car, wasn't all that bad!

Quest for the Bubble
By George J. Kimble

If you ever had to find a part
You are aware the quest is less science than art
I needed a gas gauge float
For my 1948 Chevy land boat

I had removed the tank
Cleaned it all out because it stank
Inside is a copper bubble hung on a wire loop and lever
It rides on the surface of the fuel and sends a signal, very clever

I pulled the gauge from the top
And found out that the bubble was a flop
I had a torch and some solder lead
So then I got a notion into my head

Well, resourceful as I am at doing repairs
I figured I'd solder it, and ease my cares
It seemed like an easy task
Just before the gas inside it flashed

That's when I singed my hair
My forehead was blackened and the top was bare
I can tell you now, and I am being serious
That fumes of gas and a flame is very dangerous

Now the quest was on for the bubble
I called every parts house and had the same trouble
They all listened and made the same statements
Then laughed real loud without abatement

None had ever seen one like that
After all they were mostly just young brats
Good help is hard to find these days
So I was on my way

I started out to check some junkyards
This search wouldn't be too hard
There must be hundreds of cars that used these bubbles
But every one we found had the same darn trouble

Where the wire clasped the ball
Bi-metal corrosion ate through the wall
Car after car and tank after tank
They looked just fine but they all sank

I traveled further and further a field in this quest
But every junkyard was just like all the rest
They looked good in my hand but would sink like a rock
I now had twenty of them in stock

My boy and I, from a salvage place, were returning
Along a lonesome byway we spied something burning
At closer view, it was the setting sun reflected
From the shattered glass of a car long neglected

Behind brush of cedar it was concealed
It was an Old Chevy mired above its wheels
Like mad men we leaped from our truck
And ran ankle deep through weeds and muck

The hulk was covered with rust
Mother nature was turning it back to dust
We tried to jack it up for at least an hour
But it was sunk too deep and it started to shower

In desperation I slammed my hand against the trunk
It popped open with a clunk
My son in an unusual manner
Grabbed a big claw hammer

He whacked hard and pierced the trunk floor
I encouraged him to do it a whole lot more
Finally he broke through to the rotting and pitted gas tank
Then slowly removed the top, float ball, and shank

It looked good as they all do
What was left to prove?
Hurried home and set it in a pail of water overnight
It was still floating in the morning to our delight

That float from the car bound for hell
Has served for more than 15 years in my gas tank's well
Nothing else on that wretched beast could have been used
Every part had been shot or abused

The quest for the bubble was over and success was ours
Since then we have restored several other cars
But that gem will never be forgotten
We found in the car where everything else was rotten

A Feeling Like This
By George J. Kimble

How does it feel?
To be stuck on the road
Like a road killed toad
With no plan to move the load

How does it feel?
To see cars pass you by
Without a reason why
Trying not to cry

How does it feel?
To face those expressions never changing
To hear those rods clanging
To watch smoke spew from an engine that's banging

Oh ! You were the confident one
You drove an antique for the fun
You controlled that magical force
You guided it down that winding course

How does it feel?
The anxiety that you must transcend
To make excuses and amends
To beg from your friends

How does it feel?
To impose your needs
To beg others to do deeds
To revive that smoldering steed

How does it feel?
To drag it onto a flat bed
Hooked, engine's song dead
Uncontrolled overwhelming dread

Oh! You knew it was the treasure
To make driving a pleasure
To cruise away in leisure
You took every measure

How does it feel?
To be on your own
To be all alone
With no way home
Like a motionless stone
Tell me, How, does it feel?

Poof

By George J. Kimble

It's five o'clock in the morning
It came out of the predawn darkness without warning
As I walked across the driveway all seemed natural
My wife had packed my lunch in the little brown satchel

As I opened my big Chevy's door
I made a mental note to come home early to wash my 454
That black muscle truck looked a little dirty
By now, it was pushing five thirty

When I arrived at work it was just another day
I started my routine that earns me my pay
The hustle and bustle of assigning my crews
Was interrupted by a phone call out of the blue

My wife was agitated on the other end of the line
I had to ask her to calm down several times
She was shouting about, "Where is the truck?"
The answer, I didn't have, left me dumb struck

I said sarcastically, "It's in the driveway, like it always is!"
She said emphatically, "No it is not! What kind of joke is this?"
I said, "It was there at five thirty!"
"I even noticed it was a little dirty!"

An ill sinking feeling in my cranium throbbed
The rush of realization my 454 SS truck had been robbed
Random thoughts started ricocheting around in my brain
Images of the truck flooded over with anguish and pain

Nightmares of dismemberment in some chop shop
I pleaded with her, "Have you called a cop?"
She shrieked, No she hadn't, yet
She had to get to work; she was taking my Vette.

So, Now I had to handle this thing
I dialed the police; Ring, ring, ring
I told the person on the phone
The 454 was stolen from my home

I hurried home to meet the police and had to wait
An agonizing long time considering my truck's fate
Finally, about ten, appears a police cruiser
Confidently, out steps a stern looking police officer

His questions; at first, made me feel like a suspect
By now, pacing and fidgeting, I was a nervous wreck
I described my 454 in detail; a little form he began to fill
He realized, this 454 truck wasn't just another run of the mill

I started begging him, "Please find my pick-up truck!"
"Recovery", he explained, "is a matter of luck!"
I needed some assurance from him to help me cope
But, He flatly told me, "There isn't much hope!"

He said, "I'll start an investigation"
He got in his cruiser and left without hesitation
I felt abandoned and left out to dry
I called my wife and she began to cry

The harsh reality we could not escape
We felt violated, sort of raped
Invaded, and pillaged, victimized
Frustrated, and angry, traumatized

In a stupor, I returned to work
I found myself cursing the thieving jerk
I called the insurance to stake my claim
Man, I wished I had someone to blame

Then, I guess you could call it a twist of luck
The police called and said, they had found my truck
It was found with no tires or wheels
The interior was torn up, no big deal

After some bureaucratic hassles and towing arrangements
The 454 SS was taken to a trusted repair agent
He pointed out the damage was much more extensive
And that the repairs would be much more expensive

Hauling it, wheeless, onto a roll-back
Knocked the front-end way out of whack
There were scratches and dents all over the place
The low life thieves escaped without a trace

Now, several weeks have come and gone
The repairs are moving right along
From this event we will recover and survive
We pray no more thieves invade our lives

Though, we are still feeling rather hollow
And this pill was hard to swallow
Life is strange and has many lessons to be learned
So, Don't covet material things, because POOF, they could be burned

Lifted
By George J. Kimble

I went out to Clarksville, the last show of the year
The weather was threatening, cool and rain was feared
The show was great and the trophies were grand
They even had good food at the concession stand

I left out of there smiling and happy
But the skies started looking, dark and crappy
I headed south and started down off the ridge
It started raining as I crossed Bordeaux Bridge

Now, my old Buick is a great riding car
But, when it starts raining I can't see very far
The wipers are vacuum powered, as you know
When I accelerate they just don't go

I slogged through puddles and ponding on I-65
Dodging the big trucks and trying to survive
When, there in front of me all at once
The traffic was stopped in a big bunch

Well it didn't really stop, but inched along
I entertained myself singing oldies songs
We kept this up for more than an hour
My defogger was overwhelmed by the intensity of the shower

Slogging along I was surveying the old Buick's dash
My eyes focused on the fuel gauge illuminated by a lightening flash
The pointer was sagging menacingly low
I started hoping the traffic would start to flow

The straight eight engine in my '48 Buick began to shudder
I had to pull to the shoulder with a spit and a sputter
With anticipation I tried to re-fire
That Fire Ball Eight had no more desire

Now, I was vexed and really started fuming
The rain was still pouring, but the traffic started zooming
Into the weather I slide out the passenger side
I had to go get some gas for my antique ride

I was walking, now soaked to the bone
Feeling depressed and very much alone
I finally sloshed up to a Magic Market
Probably three miles from where I had to park it

I bought a gallon of gas, the can I had to rent
Back towards the highway I quickly went
A wreck of a car with two people inside
Stopped and asked me if I needed a ride

To decline the offer, was my first reaction
But, I wanted shelter from the precipitation
I jumped into the back seat and dried my face
The car bolted forward like it was in a race

I've always said, "You can't judge the honey by looking at the hive"
But, these guys had me fearing for my life
The one driving had only three teeth and spoke with an impediment
The other looked like a tattooed fugitive, an "institutional resident"

I started worrying, filling up with strife
I hoped, before I had left I had remembered to kiss my wife
Then old toothless said, "How far? My friend!"
I replied "About three miles from the ramp's end"

When these characters saw the antique car they began to howl
Oh, I thought, now they pull their weapons and I get disemboweled
They ran up behind the Buick and came to a stop
I was mumbling a prayer to God for a passing cop

I grabbed my gas and out the door I leaped
And hollered, "Thanks for the lift", to the passenger creep
But, both got out and the biggest one said, "We will stay!"
"To help you out and be sure you are back on your way!"

I thought, Oh, They won't kill me yet, they want my keys
I was trembling from my fingertips down to my knees
I pulled the lever and opened the hood
Next to me on each side these characters stood

I primed the carb and poured the rest in the tank
Slide behind the wheel and started to crank
It took many tries before the engine tasted the gas
But, it came to life and fired at last

They jumped up and down and shouted with glee
Now, I reckoned, they could take the car and do away with me
I figured while closing the hood, I'd disappear without a trace
But, you know I never detected any malice in either one's face

I slide behind the wheel and thanked them immensely
They closed my door standing in the drizzle smiling intensely
I slipped the shifter into first and released the clutch
Leaving behind in the mist, Two Angels, by whom I had been touched

To the Bone
By George J. Kimble

We had worked all year at the research station
Way up the Ausable Chasm above the Lake Champlain Basin
Two days until Christmas, we are in the wilderness all alone
We both longed for the Holidays and the good folks at home
Weary to the bone

At supper a long silence was broken
We had decided to go home with words not spoken
She said, "We need to be rolling by first morning's light"
I said, "I'll load the Corvette tonight"
Delighted to the bone

Christmas Eve came with a crystal clear dawn
I leaped out of bed and pulled my Long-Johns on
Thirty below zero on the thermometer outside the window
I did not care I was excited and raring to go
Clear to the bone

Mentally I plotted the course we would take
West on Route three through Placid and Saranac Lake
Cross the Adirondacks over the high peaks by four
Then down into Watertown on the Ontario shore
Cut to the bone

Catch the interstate I-eighty-one
Shoot past Red Field before the setting of the Sun
Rush through Syracuse, Ithaca and past Cortland
We'd be home early, is what I had planned
Sure to the bone

As she locked the front door and pulled on a sweater
I unplugged the electric dipstick and the battery heater
I lowered the hood and closed the Corvette door
I turned the key and put my foot to the floor
Stunned to the bone

A low grumble and a moan, no ignition
In the back of my head, was this a premonition?
I called Mike, my nearest neighbor,
I said, "Bring your cables and your tractor"
Good to the bone

Like a bear leaving his den, growling my Corvette suddenly shook
A shot of ether and twenty four volts, is all that it took
You know temperatures this low turn oil into Jell-O
But, now my car was idling nice and mellow
Happy to the bone

Roads through the mountains are legend for their wrecks
None are more notorious than Rt. 3 in the Adirondacks
It is a snake coiled around many mountain breasts
It is always dangerous, and even great drivers it will test
Mean to the bone

It is picture perfect as we make our up slope flight
Beautiful Mountains covered in white
The radio guy says something about storm warnings
I switch the station. He was so boring
Dumb to the bone

She is beautiful, the cold air has reddened her checks
I am in Corvette bliss as we traverse the High Peaks
"There is no place as pretty as Lake Placid on Earth,"
She mentions the darkening sky for what it is worth
Worried to the bone

Across my windshield small droplets scurry
Little ice crystals mixed with snow flurries
Leaden sky, now, a Nor'easter does forebode
Slush is forming along the unsalted road
Soaked to the bone

It's spitting ice mixed with rain
Blast of snow screaming out of the Canadian Range
The clouds have closed down around our heads
A mountain winter storm all travelers must dread
Shaken to the bone

Our pace is drastically slowed
Visibility down to twenty feet of road
Sudden change to pure hard driven snow
Corvette wipers are working on overload
Close to the bone

Front tires struggle to maintain their grip
Rear wheels increasingly slip
Defroster can't keep the windows clear
Her face is totally inscribed with fear
Stretched to the bone

Guardrails are vanishing beneath the layers of snow
It is awfully hard to tell which way to go
We can't stop. We will be buried
I haven't been this scared since we got married
Scared to the bone

Onrushing flakes are hypnotizing
Each new slope is agonizing
Terrible crunching sounds are coming from below
As fender bergs break off from the packed snow
Pained to the bone

Slower, slower, progress measured in inches
At every new curve my partner winces
We are trapped in a clear white maze
The hood and windows are covered in icy glaze
Stuck to the bone

We have seen no other traffic
Our situation is drastic
Our nerves are all tensed
Muscles are pulsing and clenched
Stiffened to the bone

Our eyes are blurred, we're snow blind
Awful fears fill our mind
Wandering along like a fighter on dope
We press on toward the Adirondack's downward slope
Aching to the bone

It is a struggle of Nature against man and his machine
This was never a part of my wildest dream
The Corvette's wide and balanced stance
Is the only weapon giving us a chance
Muscled to the bone

We come upon a lone way station
We pull in with out any reservations
We run to the entrance through the drifted lot
We are glad to be in a place that is warm, if not hot
Frozen to the bone

Now easing up to a blazing stove
We tell the story of how we drove
Then a rumble from the road so very loud
The storekeepers say, "The road is now plowed"
Warmed to the bone

We look to our Vette and the sun magically appears
We are going home to Holiday cheer
We will follow that big old plow
We are determined, nothing will stop us now
Resolute to the bone

Destination reached, the moon shines bright on new fallen snow
Momma's house is warmly decorated and seems to glow
Everything as we always remembered it to be
Even our own stockings are hung by the tree
Beautiful to the bone

When duties or missions have for long made us roam
Blessed is the time we spend in our home
With loved ones on Christmas may no one be alone
I pray let us all be
MERRY to the bone

CHAPTER SEVEN – Show Time

Picture This	(Winter and Restoring)	- 101 -
Udn Udn Inc.	(Restoring Corvette)	- 102 -
Regina	(Trailer Queen Syndrome)	- 104 -
A Glimmer	(Car Show Experience)	- 106 -

Picture This
By George J. Kimble

Dark cloudy days, weather constantly drizzling
Garage door open slightly swaying
Yellow light shaft extending, piercing
Rock beat barely discerning
Sand paper scruffing, syncopating
Images inside wispy, moving
Old Corvette on stands, posing
Dust filled atmosphere unsettling
Hours stacked upon hours, ticking
Evenings and weekends, passing
Calendar pages slowly flipping
Bitter season begrudgingly changing
Scent of solvents, emanating.
Gray primed body, anticipating,
Compressor droning, endlessly cycling,
Nozzle spraying, menacingly hissing,
Glaze appearing, tape unmasking,
Metallic clanking, chromium bolting,
Rubber bouncing, finally rolling
Roll up chattering, slowly opening
Sunshine glaring, completely dazzling
Reflections, eye feeding, shamelessly glistening
Gestures satisfying, increasingly beaming
Darkest season expired, fruitfully bursting
New life emerging, Springtime gleefully showing

Udn Udn Inc.
By George J. Kimble

Dank darkened rain slicked streets
People live down here you wouldn't want to meet
Slowly cruising, looking for an elusive address
Lock the doors; put up the window glass
Udn udn

Finally, there on the right, a hand painted sign
The building and roll up door don't look too benign
Then appears a man with his hat all askew
Yelling, "What's up? You found us didn't you!"
Udn udn

Sliver of light appears at the bottom of the door
Crossed checkered flags painted on the warehouse floor
There is another man with a scraggly beard
My whole body is shaking; I'm feeling sort of weird
Udn udn

He comes up and taps on the window pane
I think I need a shrink to examine my brain
I pop open the door and try not to fret
That scraggly guy is slowly circling my Vette
Udn udn

I say, "Man this looks like a chop shop"
I also hope he doesn't think I'm a cop
There are cars of all models and makes
A thirty-two Chevy exposing disc brakes
Udn udn

A TPI engine hangs on a hoist
A '65 Vette body with paint still moist
Neatly arranged tools all shiny and clean
Spotless walls and everything in between
Udn udn

I spy a dyno and a jig for a frame
I feel better; I'm glad that I came
I give him my keys and admonish, "Take care of my baby!"
He says, "The Vette will be restored in three months, Maybe!"
Udn udn

Time goes by like a galloping Tortoise
Everything is done with precision and purpose
The body is finished and baked out for hours
The engine is rebuilt and dyno'd at awesome horsepower
Udn udn

This Corvette is really going to go!
It's so perfect it could win any show!
It's hard to believe, in the bowels of the city
There is a place that converts hulks into something so pretty.
Udn udn

Now if you are out cruising around
And you find yourself in the seedy part of town
You may see UDN UDN scrawled upon a door
Have no fear, You know, what that stands for
Udn udn, udn udn udn

Regina
By George J. Kimble

She sets there cool and aloof as a distant star
She draws in admirers from afar
She stands out above the rest
She poses so statuesque

Brightest hues adorn her skin so smooth
Everyone recognizes her beauty is so true
Yet there is such pity, I can tell
For the adorer of this Belle

Everyone knows the power she does possess
But alas no man will ever test
Or coax her to snarl or gyrate
That essence of force she must only emanate

Yet in her youth she did often embark
Upon long sojourns into the dark
With sensuous motion, portent of bliss
A careless abandoned flowing tryst

Still time and distance showed their strain
And her motive force wretched with pain
Stressed, cracked, aged, and spirit degenerated
Her potent youth, she longed to have rejuvenated

Then as if guided by divine presence's hand
A youthful restoration was began.
Many hours and days would pass forlorned
As bit by bit each iota was reformed.

Now in stillness of darkened bay
She awaits a judgment day
Then under veil she often goes
Upon a chariot in motionless repose

And whenever she has arrived
Her every wish is to be alive
To flare up and bellow loudly
To express her prowess proudly

Her benefactor, His fortune spent,
Now must take resolute content
Every honor he does record
The fruits of his labors are his reward

Like the phoenix from the ash arisen
This '69 Corvette will never be driven
Because she has become so esteemed
She must rein forever as the Trailer Queen

A Glimmer
By George J. Kimble

They gather there upon the green
Polishing and waxing their favorite machine
They labor intensely, over every detail they bother
The owners all act like expectant fathers

Their babies are groomed and pampered and cuddled
Heaven forbid they should encounter a puddle
They prefer the muscle cars of the past
It's such a pity they never again will go fast

Then appear some guys with badges on their chest
They are the ones who decide which beauty is best
They circle and curtsey, eyeing every aspect
They jot down notes of each little defect

Then crowds gather with green envy upon their faces
Evoked youthful memories, their mind retraces
They mention Uncle Chuck's or Cousin Jim's
He was a character, but the girls all liked him

They revel in the power of their youthful bliss
They tell their kids they used to have one just like this,
Except theirs was another color and was only a six
And for a fleeting second, the kid dreams that the Corvette is his

Now the owner's smile is wide and brimming
Because he was able to sense what the kid was dreaming
Tires were smoking and the engine was thunder
His eyes were wide and filled with wonder

Crowds will walk up and cast broad smiles
Mentally transported through time and across many miles
The hours on the field pass with a flash
The time for the trophies has come at last

The owners gather with excited anticipation
Hoping their baby is given great recognition
Regardless of judgment each owner is grinning
It's the moments, the people, that are much more than winning

CHAPTER EIGHT – Road Calls

Spring Ride	(A Corvette Club Tour)	- 109 -
Clueless	(Lost in the Mountains)	- 111 -
The Sky Is No Limit	(Corvettes Meet Airplanes)	- 114 -
Smokey Mountain Breakdown	(Car Folks Help)	- 117 -
Opportunity	(Bristol Experience)	- 119 -

Spring Ride
By George J. Kimble

The sky is a pastel blue-green
The drivers are all in their machines
Then comes the call
Let's get going y'all
We're headed for places unseen

Everyone's face is covered with smiles
Onto the street the Caravan files
Glad it didn't rain
Traffic is a pain
We go slow for the first couple of miles

Finally the last city traffic is passed
A single file is formed by the Corvettes at last
We're all out of town
The tops are all down
Now is the time to go fast

The scenery is so bucolic
In green pastures animals frolic
The farms are all splendid
The fences are all mended
True essence of life symbolic

Notice all the trees are in bloom
Along the winding road the Corvettes zoom
Up over ridges
Across little bridges
The country air smells better than perfume

Mother Nature has done her thing
Blessed us with warm breezes of Spring
Oh, so storybook
Wash the horse in the brook
On the road your Corvette is the King

The destination is a Hot Rod show
Those Hot Rods are awesome you know
The wind's in our hair
We haven't a care
We're just glad we are able to go

Our journey ends, and it's irrelevant where
What matters is, your friends were all there
All bursting with pride
It was a beautiful ride
This Corvette experience we shared

Clueless
By George J. Kimble

It's eight AM and the Corvette is all shined
He's been talking about this trip for a long time
The luggage is packed and stuffed inside
The weather doesn't matter; he's taking a Corvette ride

He hustles, hoping that he hasn't forgotten anything
He can't wait to hear those Gator Backs sing
He runs to the garage and hops into the machine
He is in a hurry to do his favorite thing

In the Corvette, he adjust the mirrors and the seat
It's forty miles to breakfast and he likes to eat
He pulls out of the drive and heads out east
The first stop is Lebanon where everyone will meet

He wishes the darn rain would just stop
He likes to drive the Corvette without the top
He hums soft and low as he tunes in the Corvette's radio
At the restaurant he spies a herd of Corvettes ready to go

Breakfast is good. It hits the spot
The eggs are just right and the coffee is hot
The usual suspects are all gathered there
One of the women is worried about the rain and her hair

He was so busy wolfing it down, He didn't ask about the route
Then someone hollered, "We're ready, It's time to pull out"
He eats one last biscuit and leaves a tip
He is really excited about making this trip

He is ecstatic, he feels mighty fine
Surveying Corvettes all in a line
He doesn't want to get lost so he pulls in behind
On the highway the Corvettes are blowing everyone's mind

He likes to drive his Corvette faster than most
The caravan is rolling at the speed the state does post
So he kicks it down and the power starts flowing
Then he remembers he doesn't know where he is going

He takes the first off ramp and at the end he waits
Smiling and giggling he thinks, "boy this is great"
Back up the on ramp he makes a quick dash
Just as the caravan starts to come past

He passes them all and laughs like a fool
Speeding and ramping he thinks this is cool
Near Cookeville the caravan stops for necessities and gas
A younger member wants to ride with him and asks

His Mom is concerned, but relents alas
Tell him, "Drive slowly", they both nod and laugh
Back onto the road the two of them jet
Now this is the way to enjoy a Corvette

After awhile they stop at a rest station
Waiting for the caravan they are very impatient
The caravan comes and they exclaim, "It's about time!"
The very next exit the Corvettes pull off in a line

The leader it seems was a little confused
When he passed the exit he thought there was two
Now the leaderless posse of shiny Corvettes
Starts off following the fool who hasn't a clue yet

Now, "you know who", is leading this group
They just didn't know he escaped from F-Troop
He doesn't know where they are going or how they'll arrive
He is just out enjoying a good morning drive

He muses to his partner, "Boy this is great"
"I don't know where to turn, so I'll just go straight"
He pulls over again and again
But the caravan follows him like chicks and a hen

Assuming they are on the right track
Tucked in behind the Corvette that is black
He wanders aimlessly like a lost pup
Hoping and praying the leaders will catch up

Luckily the true leaders find the lost pack
And finally put the caravan back on the right track
Now they arrive in Walland without any harm
To find a rustic farmhouse with plenty of charm

The sky clears up and everyone is relaxed
Dinner is served and ribs and beans are attacked
Then all good friends, the best kind of folks
Sit on the porch and tell their best jokes

Now, in the future, if you should decide
To go with this bunch on a Corvette ride
Don't worry if it is rainy or the brightest of Sun
Just remember, in a Corvette, it's the driving that is fun

Editors Note: You just had to be there

The Sky Is No Limit
By George J. Kimble

Shining fiberglass glistening in the morning Sun
Corvette drivers anticipating another day of fun
In the lot a Carnival sleeps
Onto the highway a caravan creeps

Construction slows the normal traffic
Earth movers are creating havoc
Winding very slowly along
Listening to the radio's oldies songs

Take this off ramp the CB squawks
Then there is silence and no one talks
As we pull into a field neatly cut and wide
We are hoping for a different kind of ride

We circle the Vettes into a shady nook
And leap out quick to take a look
We are greeted like a sortie coming back
From some brave mission or dangerous attack

As we enter this unusual scene
I smell the aroma of fresh baked beans
There is Bar-B-Q, cornbread and coleslaw too
A mighty fine meal to feed our crew

There are many aircraft circling and touching down
Some are colored brighter than the suit of a clown
Thundering in like eagles of prey
Wing tips tilt and gently sway

In the distance an eerie sound
A glint of light reveals a helicopter is coming down
Across this field the aircraft are strewn
And rest upon Terra this day in June

The Corvette pilots feast and delight
They drink up the sounds and the sights
They stare at huge Russian sky freighters
And ultra-lights and single-seaters

Aircraft of every use and intention
Fighters, bi-wings, and crop dusting inventions
They lift, they swoop, and they soar on high
And now the Corvette pilots are invited to come and fly

Defying the force of gravity is not a normal thing
And we fear that mother earth's pull is mightier than the wing
Coaxed on by our comrades exaltations
One by one the Corvette drivers overcome their trepidations

Now great rumbling from propeller blade
Speeding headlong across the glade
The wind buffets our small craft
Angles our wings and rudder's draft

A bump, a thump and sensations of fear
A tree line we easily clear
Excitement and wonder flood our mind
We are flying. The ground is left behind

Aloft, we spy other ships, sailing in the sea of clouds
And there is a vastness that knows no crowds
A curved horizon is majestically viewed
And planted fields are verdantly hued

In a Euphoric trance of wonder unbounded
We mock those creatures below so solidly grounded
We ogle a yellow tailed hawk floating past
From his domain we must depart alas

Now, we hurl earthward, with bodies feeling weightless
Approaching touchdown and exhaling totally breathless
As straight as an arrow with feathered crest
We touch softly earth's sweet breast

Now firmly tethered to the ground
The other Corvette fledglings gather round
We smile and beam with so much excitement
We praise our hosts for providing this enjoyment

While driving home in our Corvettes we ponder
The daring men of Kitty Hawk way back yonder
We now understand their wonderful dreams
Of gossamer wings and flying machines

Often, men dream of flying free as birds
And often they express their mind in words
As we pray before we sleep tonight
We, Thank you, kind hosts, for the freedom of flight

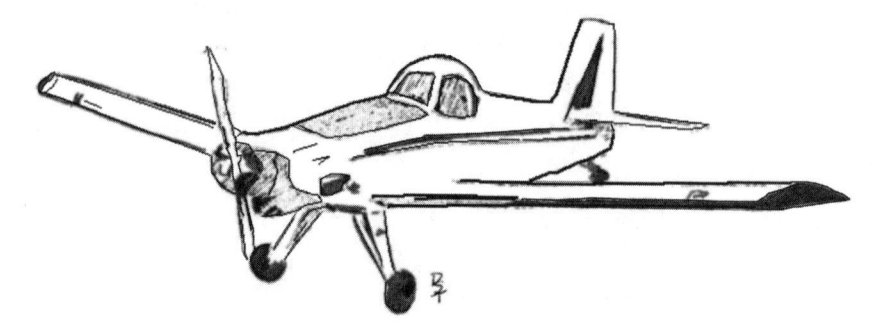

Smokey Mountain Breakdown
By George J. Kimble

It was a bright warm October day
The Corvette Caravan was well on it's way
Headed east to the Great Smokey Mountain Range
When the Mako Shark started acting strange

We were rolling in a great long line
When the Mako started falling way behind
I took an off ramp and came right back up
I ran down the Mako as it was passed by a truck

The group was now far out of sight
The driver's face was a picture of fright
I hand gestured, What is the matter?
I observed the tires and none were getting flatter

The driver pointed to her car's left rear
Then she pointed to her left ear
I dropped my glass and gave a listen
The song from her side-pipes said, the 350 wasn't missing

I saw no smoke or fluids trail
As I dropped in behind the Mako's tail
We progressed slowly, but were approaching our goal
I prayed, "Please don't let the Mako's demon take his toll"

We finally arrived at the mountain farm
It was beautiful with rustic charm
In the driveway the others were anticipating
For over an hour they had been waiting

Some of these members were here to go racing
The mechanical types were back and forth pacing
All of a sudden it was like a Nascar pit crew
A flurry of action, each member, knowing just what to do

The problem was a half-shaft on the left rear
When it was removed I heard a great cheer
A discolored u-joint revealed the true culprit
We dialed up some auto stores and one said, "We have it"

A voice said, "Now don't get too excited"
"The half-shaft and u-joint still have to be united"
"A press is needed to install the u-joint on the half-shaft"
Our caller said, "But, They have one", and we all laughed

The end of the job was like a walk in the park
Everything was fixed before it became dark
Then the Corvette Club sat down to a Bar-B-Q meal
From this event I learned a great deal

A Corvette caravan isn't like herds that roam the great plain
That abandon the weak, and those that are lame
Yes, Corvette Club members race and compete
But, We never leave a member broken down on the street

Opportunity
By George J. Kimble

Opportunity, never knocks like some believe
It whispers near the door and quickly leaves
It is a fleeting and swift coincidental convergency
When time, circumstance, and desire unite in urgency

Those who are prepared, daring, and aware
Leap upon this wispy silhouette with flair
They disregard their limiting fear
They apprehend its essence and draw it near

A slight blip upon an electronic screen
A murmur in cyber space, what did it mean?
No time to worry, No time to think
Seize the moment quick as a blink

So it came to pass in that glow of wonder
Corvettes were summoned to the Valley of Thunder
They were called to assist the Titans of racing lore
Who prepared for battle on Thunder Valley's floor

Legendary heroes would challenged these courses
In chariots of steel harnessed to multitudes of horses
They would soon guide their machines like an arrow
Down the paths of the straight and narrow

When pomp and heraldry were bestowed,
The Corvettes were called to bear the load
Transporting the gladiators before the masses,
The top contenders for each of the Dragster's classes

The spectators' screams echo in The Valley
As the feverish crews begin to rally
Sir Cory McClanathan and Sir John Force
Have now taken their posts upon the course

Demon Mustang, grotesque in proportion
Defiantly approaches the lights of caution
Abreast of him is the long fuelie rail
Exuding confidence, to never fail

The Earth quakes beneath howling dragons' claws
Flame and smoke elicits raucous applause
The lamps flash amber, then burst to green
Unleashing the spectacle of man and machine

In less than five ticks on the clock's face
We witness the conclusion of the race
300 MPH in a quarter of the mile
Provokes our faces to a colossal smile

There was a disturbance in the Force at the end
Sir Cory will live to fight again
The Force was defeated and won't return
Sir Cory had too much power to burn

Yet to our disbelief and surprise
While the night's sleep was still in our eyes
We were escorted around the back
And allowed to do hot laps on the high banked track

We were cared for in this mystical place
By a host with a special grace
Our needs were attended to with familial affection
We all, were very pleased, without exception

This experience was so fulfilling
The Corvette drivers again are willing
To take the opportunity of such grand wonder
And return to the Valley of Thunder

Thank you,
We salute you.
May the Gods Of Thunder Bless you every day
Sir Red Whitmore, of Bristol Motor Speedway

CHAPTER NINE – Doing It

Homily of The Rally Master	(Rally Start Instructions)	- 122 -
Some Like It Hot	(Autocross)	- 124 -
Rice Anyone	(A Busting One)	- 125 -
Muscle Vs. Hustle	(Mopar Beats Corvette)	- 128 -

Homily of the Rally Master
By George J. Kimble

"Hearken!" The Wicked Rally Master Pleads
"Lords and Ladies of Iron and Fiberglass Steeds
Each crook and bend alas uncharted
Will menace those not lion hearted"

"Before thee looms an adventure of epic proportion
Which hath signs of devilry and distortion
Fair thee well to enumerate and reckon
All attribute and symbol that may gravely beckon"

"You must go forth at your appointed hour
Stray not, and avoid temptation of excessive horsepower
Fortify your beings against doubtful whim
You must consummate ere the daylight falls dim"

"Though the itinerary is branched and winding,
To the pathway your oath is binding
Godspeed and safety do not forsake
Amid pestilence of traffic contemplate the brake"

"If you covet to drink from the victory chalice
Unto thyne rivals promote no malice
For each antagonist hath his own hell to pay
To toil over scrolls and documents along the way"

"Prudence 'tis eminently the surest keeper
That shields the contestant from the reaper
Yet, indecision and vacillation, plague the meek
Thus, pilots must consult navigators and wisdom seek"

"If mayhaps you are lost and filled with anguish
Unfurl the panic scabbard and extinguish
No shame will befall your grace
Others may carry the same shadow upon their face"

"Crusaders abreast your smoldering mounts
Now, Know ye, every heartbeat counts
Tarry not, while abundant clue you contemplate
Time is of the essence, do not be late"

"The quest of the byways is upon us nigh
Within thyne route no missionary can hear your cry
Into awesome sojourns, tempestuous neophytes blindly fly
Toward the marauders keep ever-watchful thyne naked eye

One second of thought 'tis oft most sly
Some, assuredly will partake of the crow baked within the pie
'Tis abject to conspire unto lies
Amass, Lords and Ladies, endeavor unto the rally your noblest try"

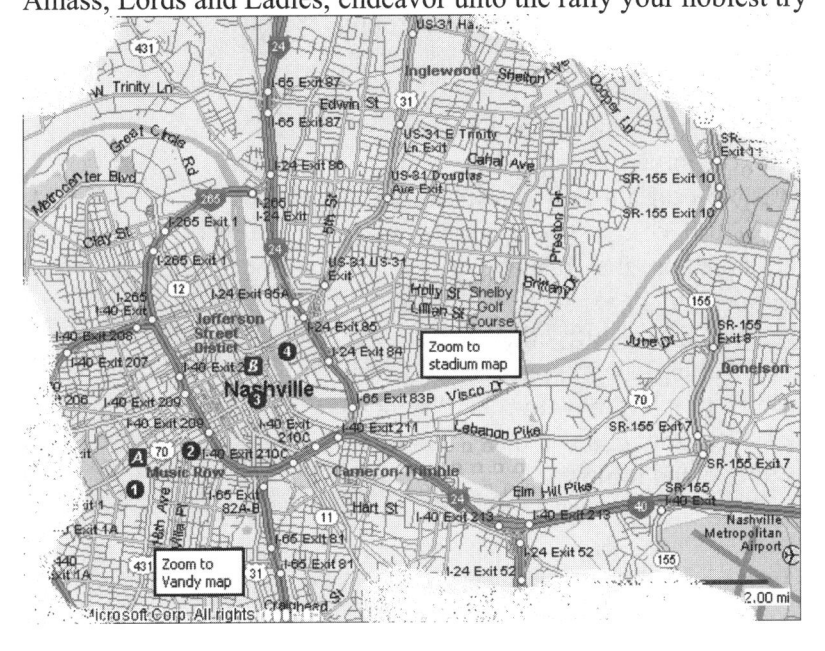

Some Like It Hot

By George J. Kimble

Blinding bright Sun
Great day for Corvette fun
Heat waves shimmering over blacktop
Small butterflies fluttering, won't stop
Air off, Five point tight
Full face secure, wait for the green light
Tached up, Deep breath, inhale
Launch! Squawl, Smoke, don't lose the tail
Brake, Heel, Toe, Gas
Up shift, turn right, pedal down, kick ass
Turn some more, brake, right pedal down
Up shift, turn in, turn out, rear end comes around
Tight gate!
Not too late
Brake, gear down, gear down, brake harder
Rumble! Smoke! Gotta drive smarter
Gas, more gas, up gear, up gear, don't swerve
Turn in, tighter, full lock, test your nerve
More power, more gas, apex reached
Break loose, Screech!
Brake, down shift, down shift, other lock,
Loud rumble, Shaking! Depressed shocks
Paste it, up shift, turn left, now turn hard right
Brake, down shift, front end is too damned tight
Turn, turn more, damn it more
Flog it to the floor
Stop! Squeals!
Now you know how a rat in a drain-pipe feels
Check time! You did all right
You are FTD, smile of delight.
Now get back in line
Try to do a better time
All this in a Parking lot
Wow, some like it Hot!

Rice Anyone?
By George J. Kimble

It was June of '89 or maybe it was '90
The weather was hot and the Sun was shiny
I had just bought the black Chevy truck
And my '89 Vette still had the new look

My son and I loaded the Vette onto the trailer
It was polished, cleaned, and under a cover custom tailored
Our destination was Bowling Green, Kentucky
To try win the Corvette Home Coming Show, if we were lucky

We arrived at our destination, Beech Bend Park
The sun was setting, it was getting dark
We dropped the Vette at the show field
Then to the camping area the truck we wheeled

Preparing to sleep there under the stars
We marveled at the vast number of Corvette cars
Hundreds parked under the shade trees
And at the gate a line as far as we could see

My, 15 year old, son was filled with fret
The perceived competition had him a nervous wreck
I consoled him, we still had one more day
The judging wasn't scheduled until Sunday

Saturday morning came covered with dew
Everything was wet even our shoes
We drove the pick-up to get something to eat
My son was still worried about the Vette getting beat

We sat near a window eating eggs and toast
The Corvettes were arriving from coast to coast
We returned to the park without making a stop
The vendors were now open and I decided to shop

Still worried my son began to wail
He might have forgotten to polish some minor detail
He ran back to the Vette and removed the cover
If anything was missed he was going to discover

He was all over that Vette like a duck on a bug
He crawled inside and vacuumed the rugs
Then in the distance we heard a roar
Like a fighter jet starting to soar

A racing Vette's burners were fully lit
I hollered,"Let's see what's up with it"
We jumped into the truck and drove to the side of the park
On our way there, we passed an original Mako Shark

My son yelled, "What's going on?", To someone who looked official
He replied, "Corvette Challenge", Quick as a whistle
Our eyes popped out, when we saw the staging lanes
My son poked me and said, "Pop, That looks kind of lame"

There in the rows of Vettes set a 300 ZX Nissan
"He should not be allowed to get in and run"
But, there were a couple of Mustangs and a GTO too
We wondered if they were going to run through

Again, the official looking guy was questioned
He said, "You can run too, just pay your admission"
My boy wanted to race our Corvette car
But, didn't want to pick up any dirt or tar

Then a light came over his face
"Let's enter the truck, it will be fun to race"
I winced but couldn't resist his look
I drove to the gate and signed the book

I said, "Okay let's give it a shot"
"Boy, if your mother finds out, she is going to be hot"
Then a guy wrote a number on my window
My son was elated, hollering, "Dad let's go!"

We were staged with an '84 Vette
I gambled a 454SS could win, But, I lost that bet
I was excited and my reaction time was poor
We finished with our bumper along side his door

Three runs against Vettes showed similar result
Then we were paired with the ZX, a final insult
"Pop", He said, "losing to Vettes that's OK"
"But, You had better blow that rice burner away"

We left the line in my usual style
He was ahead of us at the eighth mile
Each time he shifted he lost some space
When we reached the line we had won the race

We were happy as two pigs taking a dip
When we pulled up to get our timing slip
Oh, But, not the guy in the Nissan Z
He was mad as hell and screaming at me

He mentioned my ancestors from the past
And screamed that his Z was supposed to be fast
Getting smoked by a truck was such a crock!
Then I told him it was pure stock

Now, On Sunday our Vette won it's class
Our aim for a great weekend had come to pass
The show judges presented us with a great plaque
But, The rice burner's loss was what we talked about all the way back

Many years have came and went
Off to college my son was sent
Still when we see a 300 Z machine
We wonder at the people who don't drive the American Dream

Muscle Vs. Hustle
By George J. Kimble

Friday night, five o'clock traffic, Its all jammed
I'm in a hurry. I'll be damned
I'd like to know the name of the stupid jerk
That laid out the plan for this interstate work

I've pointed my Corvette north out of Nashville
I have a date with a road course near Louisville
There is a ton of prep on race day
I do this for the glory not for the pay

I test, I tune, and tires I try
I tweak and adjust to beat the other guy
I want to get there tonight and get some sleep
This line of behemoths is moving at a glacial creep

Three hundred and forty horses under my hood
All that power, and it is doing me no good
Oozing along at a three mile per hour clip
On the horizon the sun is starting to dip

To the right I see a ramp and decide to gamble
Up the darkened exit slowly I ramble
I am not alone when I come to the stop
There is an old Mopar in primer and a ragtop

He turns to the right with a chirp
I think hurry up, Mopar don't be a jerk
This dark road is narrow, but I'm ready to pass
He lays down rubber and I smell fumes of gas

I keep his winged tail close to my hood
One of his taillights doesn't work too good
This road is very curvy and not well lit
As I narrow the gap he gives the pedal another hit

We go on like that for several miles
I start to appreciate his driving style
He looks ahead to see if the bends are clear
He crosses lanes and onto the shoulder often veers

This all reminds me of an episode at Watkins Glen
I was just a puppy way back then
I was peddling a 1958 Corvette
Another and I snuck onto the track to settle a bet

My nemesis was a Dodge powered by a Hemi
What I lacked in power, He lost in heavy
I chased him around and around that closed track
He skillfully used it all and kept me in back

Now, this was different because I have plenty of muscle
Everyone knows about Corvettes cornering in a hustle
While handling advantage, now, might be mine
He is a local, and he knows the best line

I chase and dip and nearly rub his rear
I'm glued so tight I can see him smile in his mirror
He's driving, like a Matador. He has no fear
I'm tossing and turning and using every gear

Miles slip by like a midnight dream
That ol' Hemi roars like an assassin's scream
Suddenly we burst onto a straight
I catch sixth gear, the speedo says one thirty eight

I felt he let me pass him, I didn't know why
There was an upcoming ninety screaming slow down or die
I down loaded the gears in one hell of a hurry
My Corvette began to shudder like a ship in a fury

He dropped to the inside and, in a glance, was past
Though better equipped, in this two-car race, I was last
The Corvette technology saved me from disaster
But, his experience and knowledge crowned him the master

I settled down and began to follow
My Corvette pride I had to swallow
We came to fork, I took left, and he took right
I flashed my high beams, as a salute, to the best driver that night

CHAPTER TEN – Zoom Zoom Zoom

Heroes of The Mud	(Dirt Track Memories)	- 132 -
The Test	(Racing Grand Sport)	- 134 -
A Different Battle Scene	(Mosport Race)	- 135 -
Expedition	(Le Mans Race)	- 137 -
The Winner That Lost	(Racer Killed)	- 139 -
Circuit Rap	(The lady's Pit Crew)	- 141 -
Super Stock Racer	(Aged Race Drivers)	- 142 -

Heroes of The Mud
By George J. Kimble

Late fifties and early sixties
There were places oh so nifty
Little rings wound so tight
They ran the dirt on Saturday night

Remove the fenders and blueprint the block
Weld up a roll cage and call it stock
Lots of iron front and back
Local heroes run these tracks

Groove their tires to get some bite
Brightest paints stand out at night
No big sponsors in their story
These guys run, just for glory

Quarter mile tracks in the dirt
Big men wearing jeans and T-shirts
Places where young men get their start
Lust of victory in their hearts

At locales like Dunkirk and Waterloo
These men had their battles to do
Earl Bodine and Jackie Soaper,
And Chubby Chandler at Chemung were super

Selins Grove, Towanda and Dundee
Just plain folks would come to see
The great racers of the U.S.A.C. circuit
Irish Jack Murphy, Noland Swift and Harry Pruitt

I was just a small boy then
But every day I longed for the weekend
Pop, big brothers and I would go
Then ol' "39" behind the Buick we would tow

He picked the number like Jack Benny
Pop was past that age and plenty
Younger men drove his cars
A couple of them became big stars

One young man I recall
Who seemed a notch above them all
He won the championship in modified stock
That man was called Gordon Johncock

My fondest season was when Pop built the Eagles
These were cars with rear engines that were "legal"
Spoiler up front and wing in back
These were built for the Macadam tracks

Now I turn on the TV and watch my Heroes' kids
Speed around the tracks and try not to skid
These are the great drivers of Nascar
Man this sport has gone so far!

My friends looked up to baseball stars
And couldn't fathom what I saw in those cars
They probably thought I was a dud
All my Heroes played in the mud

As sure as God made men from clay
I remember those golden days
Dirt tracks are in my blood
And all my Heroes were made from mud

The Test
By George J. Kimble

Like vultures around and around they circle that track
Nittering, nattering, a darting attack
So many growling, howling, competitors a pack
The Jackals, the Jaguars, the Cobra that spat

Pieces and parts disemboweling some
Blistering tiger paws and on they run
From high noon past the setting sun
The chase will grind on until one day is done

The Porsches scrambled and shrieked and spun by the side
The Ferraris, like a prancing horse in fits, just died
Lotus and Mercedes on turn one, in flames collide
Through anguish and smoke and debris one Corvette did slide

Like a glistening gem on a sand laden coast
Daytona's road straights and sinews demand the most
Endurance of twenty-four hours, the banners menacingly boast
As the flags of checkered unfurl, all but a few will be just ghosts

On the altar in front of racing's majestic court
On the podium arises the king of this sport
From lands and countries afar, the enthusiasts exhort
The winner, the champion, the blue and white Corvette Grand Sport

A Different Battle Scene
By George J. Kimble

In 1966 we took a little trip
Across the Canadian border to the province of Quebec
We took a little oil, and we took a little gas
And we took some Good Year tires, and we took a little cash

The "General" said, "We could take 'em by surprise"
If those tires would stick, and we didn't try to slide
Ol' Mosport was a really slippery track
So we mounted up some rain slicks, and made another lap

About this time, the rain was pourin' down
We doubled up the wipers, and made another round
Bumps in the corners started shakin' things all loose
Our left rear shock nearly brained a grazing moose

Through three more turns our Corvette had to limp
We were caught on TV, with pictures from the blimp
We didn't know for sure how bad was the bust
On a loyal pit crew, we had to lay our trust

We pitted real quickly, when it began to thumpin'
Everyone else got out kinda slow
We started passin' Porsches like they weren't a runnin'
We didn't believe, that was as fast as they could go
We ran through the esses, and we ran through the corners,
And we ran through the nineties, where the Jags couldn't go
We ran so fast that we began a lappin'
The fans all said, "We were puttin' on a show"

We pulled into second as a Lotus left the road
It flipped and it flopped and it looked just like a toad
And the team for them Porsches was all set to crow
When the white flag dropped with one more lap to go

On his rear bumper, we set the Grand Sport's sights
And just kept pullin' closer, through the left and rights
We stretched out our necks, to see the pit board sign
As the two battlin' heroes came across the line

We roared o'er the hills and down through the hollow
We gave it all we had 'cause we didn't want to follow
The margin of victory surely was real thin
As our Corvette passed him just in time to win

If you can't remember this little bit of history
The legends of Grand Sports might be just mystery
We asked for no mercy and gave out no pity
Maybe you'll remember the Grand Sports, from this little ditty

So we fired our engines and we kept on a racin'
And there wasn't any tracks where we wouldn't go
We ran at Le Mans and we ran down at Sebring
And we even ran a race down in ol' Mexico
And we ran so fast that nothin' could catch us
And the fans came to see, our Vettes puttin' on a show

Expedition
By George J. Kimble

From an ideal, a team was fashioned
Dedicated to racing with a passion
Four hardy soles, four men of action
To challenge the world, would be their satisfaction

They knew that there wasn't much time
They had to hurry to complete their design
Respect for American cars was in decline
They'd race in Europe from England to the German Rhine

At events like Karlskoga, Le Mans and Nurburgring
The winners were Mercedes, Lotus and Citron things
So onto the Continent, a Corvette they would bring
Confident the Corvette could deliver a sting

They worked many nights, their fingers to the bone
They painted the Corvette blue and white two-tone
With no factory help, they were on their own
The first big race was to be Silverstone

With no time for testing, they would tempt their fate
To face Moss, and Villeneuve and the legendary greats
Onto a boat, the Corvette was packed in a crate
Then because of customs, the car arrived late

Depressed, they left England and headed to France
On the Continent, no one gave them a glance
All the big boys didn't even give them a chance
They weren't waltzing Matilda. This was the big dance

On they pressed to improve the car
They tuned the suspension with a larger sway bar
Bigger brakes were mounted so they could stop hard
Then vents were ducted behind the tires

Bolted on Koni shocks to make it more stable
And a 37-gallon tank was mounted with aircraft cable
Now at Le Mans they were ready and able,
As they filled out the papers at the registrars table

A sleek machine of exceptional grace
Radically modified to win the race
In the time trials it set the pace
The Corvette was driven by an Ace

During the race, their confidence was growing
Twelve hours down and the Corvette was still going
After dark, one headlight stopped glowing
They finished the race without anything blowing

American pride swelled up in their chests
With a great honor, they had been blessed
All the Europeans humbly confessed
That mighty Corvette had them impressed

Now it was long ago in 1960
That Corvette team performed with such dignity
American daring against European Society
I tip my hat and salute the Corvette team Camoradi

The Winner That Lost
By George J. Kimble

It all got started when he was very young
He was a competitor marching to a different drum
He was something, a phenomenon on wheels
He was blessed with a touch, a natural feel

He started out winning, driving a go-cart
He was ruthless, a predator at heart
At age 16, he drove his first sprint
He won everything, everywhere he went

No sponsor would back him or give him a deal
He was an intimidator; he had no public appeal
Traveling the country, he beat the local heroes on their own track
He ignored their jeers and even painted his car black

He was a nightmare; the fans loved to hate
He came to your track intending to dominate
He would spin a few hot laps at a torrid pace
Then at the end, he would sling mud in your face

He won in the Northeast and he won out West
His reputation was growing; they called him the best
Romance was not part of his tortured dreams
He dreamed of winning in his racing machine

Like a bounty hunter the circuits he would roam
All the time he prowled, solitary, alone
No helpers, no soul mate, no place to call home
Never a smile or kind word at any speed drome

Then it happened, His life was forever changed
He noticed a girl smiling and felt very strange
He never saw anyone do that before
She came to the pits and knocked on his trailer door

Whereever he went on his racing mission
She would suddenly appear like an apparition
Although he kept driving and winning often
His technique was changing; his style had softened

While towing his racer in a driving rain
A careless driver crossed into his lane
He tried to avoid it, but the tires slipped
The trailer he was towing turned and flipped

There was no witness, and no one to blame
The trooper at the scene, said it was the rain
It was reported, in the newspaper, near the back
An unknown driver was killed leaving the racetrack

The girl's sister found her reading and crying
She said she loved him, and she wasn't lying
I don't know, but I'm fairly sure
His style had changed because he loved her

When I'm at the track and the race is called due to rain
I choke back tears and try to clear my brain
His drive to win had an awful cost
But most of all I mourn her loss

He won everything except his fate
He never kissed her; they never did date
Now she cries whenever it rains
Because she is the only one that remembers his name

Circuit Rap
By George J. Kimble

No tell, Motel
Slick Chick,
Puttin' on lipstick,
Back step, gotta prep
Pullin' on a dip stick
Nightmares, who cares
Outta the groove, bust a move
Too tight, too loose
Pit crew, that's you
Speed kills, gives her thrills
No sweat, you bet, no regret
Motor drones, girl moans, you're alone, call home
Pack it up. Pack it in
Take her best shot. Try to win
Tires turn, rubber burns, you learn
You cry, mystified, she likes another guy
Road show, gotta go, no time for the ho'
Saturday night, wound tight, Bullring, another fight
Banked steep, dive in deep, She beat the other creep
Checkered flag, what a drag, you're still dancin' stag
Heart's broke, life's a joke, recalculate bore and stroke
No glory, simple story
Just a wrench, on the bench
Loose lug, no hug, let her go with a shrug
Off course, no remorse
Hit the wall, awful force
No tell, Motel
Her racing thing has gone to hell

Super Stock Racer
By George J. Kimble

Way up in New York's evergreen woods
A trailer up on blocks, precariously stood
Out in the yard lay several cars
A couple looked like they fell from Mars

Rusting and battered hulks from the past
Everyone out there with busted glass
Little of creature comfort around this place
This is not about trailer trash, but about a man born to race

He could drive anything with wheels
Around here, he's what they call, "The Real Deal"
"That boy would race anything from the time he was small"
"Bicycles, tractors, dirt bikes, go carts, he raced them all"

He was sixteen when he went to work in a lumber yard
He didn't like the work, it was too damned hard
The boss saw him racing a forklift and he got fired
He told his daddy, that he had just retired

He had nothing, not a penny to his name
Somehow, he figured racing would be his claim to fame
Pastures, fields, dirt tracks, short tracks, high banks, paved
Everywhere he went the folks just raved

Along about then some folks with big time money
Decided they would recruit "Little Brownie"
They hired the best mechanics and built up a team
They constructed for him, a Super Stock Racing Machine

It had a sponsor's name on the side
Little Brownie had a big time ride
He was a competitor, so lion hearted,
He was always in the money, no matter where he started

Drive hard, deep into the turn
Never give a thought of crash and burn
He was amazing, cunning, and daring
To him the lead, wasn't at all, about sharing

He ran World of Outlaws, then Silver Crown
Open wheeled machines, world renowned
He lapped the country on hundreds of tracks
He was a success and would never look back

But time and age are the same for every man
They respect nobody's plan
The edge gets dull and harder to find
Those wrecks and injuries start to haunt the mind

As he aged, his skills became more corroded
His sponsor's love for him slowly eroded
On the circuit, he was distinguished
His fire is low, but not extinguished

His eyes sparkle; his head is gray and his body frail
And to any passerby, he will tell his tales
He will tell you, as around the yard he limps
He saw fame, but just a glimpse

He told me this and I'm sure he knows
"A racing life is a hard row to hoe"
"Some end up healthy"
"Some even end up wealthy"

"Some just slowly fade away"
"Some even leave a family to grieve and pray"
As he speaks, it all becomes abundantly clear
He followed his dream for many, many years

He pulls up a rocker, to lighten his load
Love for Brownie was an Oval Road
Seated on his porch, next to a broken down AMC Pacer,
Is what remains of "The Super Stock Racer"

CHAPTER ELEVEN - Life, Liberty and Pursuit

Spinning Out Of Control	(Need a Fast Car)	- 145 -
Defeat The Sinister Ones	(C-5R Is To Win)	- 147 -
Last Chance For Sunoco	(It Was Done)	- 149 -
Specter	(Devil Racing)	- 151 -
Ain't It A Shame	(Bad Wreck Kids)	- 152 -
Walking	(Corvette Brag)	- 154 -

Spinning Out Of Control
By George J. Kimble

We just met
Long brown hair
Ain't nobody's pet
Lips to share
Got no roots yet
Just don't dare
Feeling much regret
We can't be a pair

    I gotta run far
    I need a fast car
    A Corvette will do
    I gotta leave you

Looks that kill
Open arms just waiting
A body to thrill
Charms so intoxicating
Great woman's skills
My heart's palpitating
All gives me chills
I'm hesitating

    I gotta run far
    I need a fast car
    A Corvette will do
    I gotta leave you

Your eyes so blue
Many chances taken
Your smile so true
Many words unspoken
If I touch you
Seems love is a token
I'll stick like glue
Many hearts get broken

  I gotta Run far
  I need a fast car
  A Corvette will do
  I gotta leave you

To Defeat the Sinister Ones
By George J. Kimble

They've built a car of great report
To defeat the sinister ones
It's been the dreams of many young men
And God I know I'm one

Its mother was a mechanic, the tuner of great machines.
Its father is a driver, the heart of every team.
The only thing a driver needs, is luck and a track.
And the only time he is satisfied, is when he leads the pack.

There is a world challenge, to race the Sinister Ones
A test of great endurance, to crown the Champions
People, I'm here to tell you, go ahead and place your bets.
At Le Mans, the world will be stunned, by the Racing Corvettes.

Now, Mothers tell your children,
Don't lose hope, as some have done.
Chevy has built a race car,
To defeat the Sinister Ones

The Porches and Ferraris, are all battle dressed
For too many seasons, they have been called the very best.
They unfurl their flags, and the victor's spoils they claim.
They give no mercy on the track, and rivals they put to shame

The spirit, of the warrior, is hardened under fire.
Racing Corvettes are historic, to legends the Corvette aspires
In sports car battles, there is everything to gain.
This, conquest of the world, must end in Victory Lane.

Oh, Mothers show your children,
A vision of things to come
A great battle for the Corvette,
To defeat the Sinister Ones

And, Mothers tell your children,
To believe in what's been done.
Believe the Corvette Racer,
Will defeat the Sinister Ones

Last Chance for Sunoco
By George J. Kimble

Long line of headlights, into my eyes glare
Long way down the road and she just don't care
Long time now, her battery light glowing red
Long argument and I can't believe what she said

One last smoke on the passenger's seat
One rod knocking, will it overheat?
One more mile of sadness
One man lost in midnight madness

Last exit, caustic green glow
Last thought, is she going to blow?
Last heart beat, feels abnormally slow
Last chance for Sunoco

Long road, twisted leaving
Long life, happiness and sorrow weaving
Long pondered, finally deciding
Long yellow lines, highway dividing

One old song, on the radio playing
One soul lost and saying
One thought in my mind is staying
One sputter and cough, tank empty, betraying

Last sense of power gone
Last wish to see the dawn
Last station light, faintest glow
Last chance for Sunoco

Long ramp fills my view
Long love, Is it through?
Long gray bus coming through
Long way overdue?

One minute yes
One minute no
One minute stay
One minute go

Last drop of gas and dollar spent
Last spark from the battery rent
Last memory as I watched her go
Last chance for Sunoco

Long passage of lover's fight
Long kiss, something's not right
Long vivid dreams and cold sweat nights
Long look into head-on lights

One circuit disrespecting
One mind disconnecting
One for another, heart beseeching
One spark, but cables not reaching

Last drop of oil pressure
Last throb of sensual pleasure
Last sign said, " SLOW"
Last Chance for Sunoco

Specter

By George J. Kimble

I went down to Georgia; Road Atlanta was the place
It was late at night. I was preparing my Corvette for a race
I was mixing up some nitro, when a specter did appear
He was ugly as sin, something mortals are bound to fear

He said, "I am a driver, the best you've ever seen"
Smoke and sparks came out his ears and places in between
He said, "I'll bet your Corvette; My Firebird will burn your tires off"
But, I wasn't scared, Because my Corvette has never ever lost

He jumped inside his Firebird; it began to howl
I cranked up my Corvette, with a mighty growl
Then lightening struck, and flames outlined the course
I had no fear, since my Corvette was an awesome force

That red car took off, like a bat out of hell
The awful stench of rubber burning, was all that I could smell
I knew he meant business, and this wasn't just for fun
But, my Corvette jumped out, like it was shot from a gun

I chased him round the bends, and closed in on the straights
We were neck and neck, when we reached the timing gates
I looked over at his face, as we screamed down a rise
That is when I noticed, he had fire in his eyes

I knew the approaching corner, only had one groove
He wasn't going to let up, and I wasn't going to move
Then at the ninety, we both did arrive
There is an awful sound, when two racers do collide

He spun off the road, in a ball of fire and smoke
I pulled into the pit, and not a word was spoke
Many races have come and gone, since that eerie night
Every time I pass a red car, I still recall that sight

If you are driving out there, and it is late at night
If you see a red Firebird, and headlights seem too bright
You are riding in your Vette, and get a little fright
Take this as a warning; be sure to dim your lights

Ain't It A Shame
By George J. Kimble

Mike and Harry
Looking kinda scary
Coming down the turnpike
Probably should have hitch hiked

Muscle car and Corvette
Racing on a big bet
Corvette's stroking,
Muscle car is smoking

Think of two friends
Rushing towards a sudden end
No shame in a car duel
Shame never occurs to young fools

Side by side
Muscle car starting to slide
Control is slipping
To the ragged edge they're ripping

Get up, set up
Some one better let up
We all believe in dumb luck
But, No one saw the dump truck

Tires squeal
Crumpled steel
Gas tanks do explode
Blood's all over the road

Crash in, Bashed in
No one would give in
Two kinds of death wish
One kind of cold fish

I know, You know
Sometime, We'll all have to go
But, When two young men die
Makes a grown man want to cry

No Blame, stupid game
Everything is up in flame
Well anyway, the reaper came
I say, "Ain't It A Shame"

Walking
By George J. Kimble

You keep saying you've got something for me
And you keep saying you've got something tough
Well, I'm not shaking and you don't scare me – Yeah!
And my Corvette may look a little rough

"Cause this Vette was built for racing
And that's just what it's gonna do
This Vette was built for racing
And it's gonna walk all over you

And you keep bragging all about your Ford car
Like it's the only thing upon the track
And you won't believe the Bow Tie is the star - Yeah!
I just keep saying, "Put up a little Jack"

'Cause this Vette was built for racing
And that's what it's gonna do
This Corvette was built for racing
And it's gonna walk all over you

Now the time has come for you to show me
And It's time for that blue oval to pay it's dues
We are staged and lights are flashing on the tree - Yeah!
 And I hope Ol' Henry taught you to sing the blues

'Cause this Vette was built for racing
And that's just what it's gonna do
This Corvette was built for racing
And it's gonna walk all over you

Lots of smoke and the smell of tires burning
At the line, that is your normal deal
And my Vette simply starts it's tires turning - Yeah!
Just a little chirp or maybe a tiny squeal

"Cause Vette was built for racing
And that's just what it's gonna do
This Corvette was built for racing
And it's gonna walk all over you

After all that talk and your loud braggin'
My Corvette was on top at the end
And maybe you should trade for a station wagon -Yeah!
And I hope you learned a lesson my dear friend

'Cause this Vette was built for racing
And that's what it's gonna do
This Corvette was built for racing
And it just walked all over you

FINISH

About The Author

George J. Kimble was born in 1949 in Upstate New York to a family that loved racing. The family was involved with mostly dirt track racing. George's father built cars that ran, in those days, as stockcars. He spent many weekends with his family, of four brothers and two sisters a stepbrother and eight stepsisters, at venues like Shangri-La, Bath, Waterloo, Oswego, and Chemung, New York. His memories include his mother driving in "Powder Puff Derbies", cheering on his stepfather Ed's cars. Hanging around the drivers and often helping prepare the cars for the next race. He spent long hours with his brother John laying in bed and looking out the window to the street below identifying the cars that went by. He has loved cars since he was a tot.

George was married to, his wife in 1972, the former Carol Comfort. They have one son, Eli, who has spent many hours with George restoring antique cars and showing Corvettes. George, Carol and Eli have a deep appreciation for the automotive hobby and the people that make it so interesting.

George is involved with several Corvette and Antique car clubs in the region around Middle Tennessee. His cars have earned local, regional and national awards. The experiences he has had, with the people, auto clubs, car shows and racing, inspired him to write the poetry in this book. Several years ago he was nicknamed "The Road Poet".

George served in Viet Nam and earned a degree from The State University of New York at Plattsburg in Environmental Science. George has worked in Nashville Tennessee for the past twenty-seven years.